The Pass(ed)over Table

Reawakening the Healing Balance of Grace and Truth in Communion

By Michael S. Wolff

Copyright © 2025: All rights reserved Credits

The Pass(ed)over Table
Published by: Reconnections, Inc.
ISBN# 979-8-9863874-8-2
Copyright © 2025 by Michael Wolff

Cover design by Elaina Lee,
www.forthemusedesign.com

All rights reserved. Non-commercial interests may reproduce portions of this book without the express written permission of the author, provided the text does not exceed 300 words. When reproducing text from this book, include the following credit line: "The Pass(ed)over Table" by Michael Wolff. Used by permission."

Commercial interests: No part of this publication may be reproduced in any form, stored in a retrieval system, or transmitted in any form by any means—electronic, photocopy, recording, or otherwise—without prior written permission of the author, except as provided by the United States of America copyright law.

Scripture quotations are taken from the New American Standard Bible®, Copyright © 1960, 1962, 1963, 1968, 1971, 1972, 1973, 1975, 1977, 1995 by The Lockman Foundation. Used by permission. (www.Lockman.org). All definitions of Hebrew and Greek words are taken from Strong's Exhaustive Concordance (1980, Abingdon Press, and PC Study Bible for same (1995, Biblesoft)

Printed in the United States of America

Michael may be contacted via email at Reconnectedchurch@gmail.com, Website: www.Theawakenedchristianman.org

Table of Contents

Introduction v
I.   What to do With Life's Storms 1
II.   Whatever Happened to the Passover? 13
III.   To Unbelievers and Believers 34
IV.   Recognizing Sin 43
V.   A Love to Embrace / An Admonishment to Consider 58
VI.   Prodigals, Fathers, and Brothers 71
VII. The Soma: The Body of Christ 86
VIII. The Matthew 5 Alternative 101
IX.   Ministering and Experiencing Admonishment 117
X.   The Best Confession 131
XI.   Et tu, Judas? 142
XII. The James 5 Gathering 150
XIII. Walking Through a Powerful Ceremony 168

XIV.	Bringing It Back to the Church	181
XV.	It's up to You Now	185
Appendix A: Leadership Teaching & Preparation Outline		191
Appendix B: Prayer Recorder		197
Appendix C: The Communion/ 12-Step Comparison		199

Introduction

Early in my walk of faith, the Spirit led me to begin to wonder why a ceremony that seemed to hold the power of health, life, and even death in the early church had been reduced to 5–10-minute, ritualistic rather than impactful, observances. Up until that time, like a good churchgoer, I just went through the motions like everyone else without truly understanding its meaning, purpose, or the power it held.

I found myself leaving Communion services feeling no different than I did when I walked in, and as God led me to watch, I noticed the same reaction from most of those around me. Something was missing. Something God put there had been passed over in the way we had come to do it. The Spirit was calling me to find a deeper meaning than I had sought up to that time. I can only say, when it comes to the message you will find in these pages, what Paul said concerning the source of his Epistles, "For I neither received it from man, nor was I taught it, but I received it through a revelation of Jesus Christ" (Gal. 3) is true. Were it not for the initial conviction something was amiss concerning such a widely accepted way of participating, and the revelations the Spirit gave me to record here, I would still 'just be doing it' like everyone else.

He led me to throw out all my traditional understandings and turn fresh eyes upon the Passover of the Exodus, the actions and words of Jesus at His Passover, the practices of the Pentecostal Church in Acts, and the instructions of Paul in 1st Corinthians. At the time, I was privileged to be discipling a group of very special high-schoolers, and as I shared what God was showing me with them, we started experimenting with what became the process you will read about in *The Pass(ed)over Table*. I could not have done it without them and their youthful openness to new ideas.

Through trial and error, we found Communion was our regular therapy session with God—a ceremony full of power to root out the 'chaff' the enemy constantly plants in our wheat fields, thereby maintaining our state of emotional and spiritual well-being. People were being set free and healed from the effects of protracted periods where covered-up sin and hidden emotional baggage were carried. But we discovered those who wanted to discover Communion's power would have to come to seek more than just its comforts. They would also have to be willing to accept the often-daunting challenges the One who came to us 'full of grace *and* truth' imposed upon everyone He touched. In the greatest gift He gave to His body, that would include doing an objective and transparent self-examination, confessing sins to God and man, and then being obedient to whatever He prescribed as the remedy.

We came to find the 'knife' of self-examination, confession, and action was what had been passed over in the pursuit of the comforts of grace, and the table needed to be reset to include it if we wanted to reawaken Communion's power! When we did, we discovered returning to a biblical Communion ceremony contained a power to bring our rag-tag band of misfit kids together in unity, and bond them in love, that surpassed our wildest expectations! If it did this for us, it can also do it for your fellowship, but you must restore what has been passed over. You must re-employ the knife!

This book seeks to take you, the administrators of God's most holy ceremony, back in time to a powerful, life-changing event that has been largely lost to the modern church and desperately needs to be rediscovered. But Communion's power will only be reawakened if you remove the blinders, set aside any preconceived notions you may have as to how it's supposed to be done and what it's supposed to accomplish, and take a fresh look at it. I hope you will, for I believe lives literally depend upon it.

Chapter I
What to do with Life's Storms

> "Life is filled with detours and dead ends,
> trials and challenges of every kind."
> — Russell M. Nelson

Life is full of storms. Sometimes, these tempests are thrust upon us and sometimes we create them ourselves. Regardless, the certainty remains that Christians—even the most sincere and dedicated ones—must endure chaos from within and without in this life. Ironically, this is not a bad thing because it is through learning to endure trials in faith that James tells us we find the perfection God seeks for us (Jas. 1).

Given that these squalls are inevitable and even profitable if handled well, we are left with two choices as to what to do when the clouds begin to gather and toss about what were formerly serene seas. We can let them sink us or learn how to pilot our ships deftly through them to safety and new understanding. The storms of life aren't the issue as much as how we endure them, and what sort of people they ultimately lead us to become in the end. The Bible tells us that even the Son of God 'learned through the things He suffered' (Heb. 5), and so suffering is both inevitable and profitable.

The effects of our storms will help mature and guide us, and the collateral damage they cause to others around us can be reduced or eliminated, if we take hold of the rudder of our ships and learn how to navigate through them with skill, integrity, and purpose. However, they can also become deadly whirlpools that suck us in and drown us if we allow them to. At that point, the storms take the rudder, become the forces that navigate our lives, and we become hapless passengers on our own 'Titanics.'

The key to piloting our ships through these storms effectively is to acknowledge they exist, remain humble and repentant, keep our eyes upon the Lighthouse of our faith and, walking with the Holy Spirit, maintain an enduring, consistent course to calmer seas. As long as we keep the prow headed directly into the wind and waves, they may rock us, but they will not capsize us. That means incurring a certain amount of discomfort, as navigating storms always will. But, sadly in the modern church, we have become far more interested in appearances than substance and far more consumed with turning away from conflict than steering into it. We ignore the Spirit's call to deal with our issues and then rationalize away the warning signs because, in the short term, it seems so much simpler and far less painful.

When we do that over an extended period of time, short-term solutions lead to what the Bible calls dangerous 'practices.' If we keep up these practices long enough, we can fall into the most insidious of all traps for believers: numbness and lukewarmth resulting in the superficial and hypocritical lifestyles that categorize far too many in the pews today. If we continue to ignore God's persistent warning signs, we become lost in a twilight zone of proclaiming we are one thing while, in actuality, living in an entirely different way. It is this very thing that unbelievers observe in the church and mock, witnessing instances of worldly living among churchgoers paralleling those in their own world.

Knowing we're slipping under the waves, and yet feeling powerless to do anything about it, either capsizes us or something within awakens and seeks a solution. We realize that, under our strategies, we've lost our direction and therefore need help finding our way out. We know that without the sure hand of God and the help of the fellowship to restore us to safe havens, we will end up drowning. The good news is God has given us a special ceremony specifically to bring darkness to light, and to be healed and set free from cover-ups and the hypocrisy that results. This book is about reawakening that sleeping giant!

Where the Knife was Lost

Would it be so wrong to infer that somehow the institutional church could have misinterpreted something over which there seems to be such universal agreement? How could it be that I stand against so many well-educated, well-intentioned church leaders and raise a red flag over something as accepted as our current model of Communion? This is a question I asked myself when God caused me to take a deeper look. Was it Him, or me, that was causing me to swim this far from the mainstream of conventional practice?

At the beginning of the book of Revelation, Jesus offers His seven churches both praise and warning. He even threatens to 'remove their crowns and lampstands' from before His throne if they fail to repent. Did they get something wrong? When He came, what caused His total focus and mission on earth to be to 'the lost sheep of the House of Israel?' Not the gentiles mind you, but God's children lost in God's own house! Had the religious leaders of His day who had led them astray gotten something wrong? Did He enter the homes of sinners with a whip and fire in His eyes, overturning the tables of the merchants in the public square as He did when He entered His Father's own house? Who stoned the prophets and crucified Christ—the unbelievers?

Who did Jesus constantly battle with if not the keepers of accepted theological thought? Who has God sent His prophets to throughout time to rebuke for distorting and perverting His message? Who but the keepers of the institutional 'popular' church have sought to supplant faith with religion down through history? Religion always follows faith. It is 'the tares among the wheat' (Matt. 13) that always spring up where good seed is sown, but that God allows to grow for our testing and perseverance. When Jesus walked the earth, it was those who said, "We see" (John 9), but whom He called 'blind guides' who had gotten it all wrong, so to say the same can't be true today would be a real stretch. And so, I believe I stand on firm biblical ground to say, "Oh yes, the keepers of religious doctrine can, and do, get it wrong."

Lastly, what did the keepers of popular religion do with all the ceremonies God entrusted them with? Isaiah 1 sums it up well, "What are your multiplied sacrifices to Me?...I have had enough...Bring your worthless offerings no longer...I cannot endure iniquity and the solemn assembly... They have become a burden to Me and I am weary of bearing them. So when you spread out your hands in prayer, I will hide My eyes from you. Yes, even though you multiply prayers I will not listen...Wash yourselves, make yourselves clean, and remove the evil of your deeds from My sight. Cease to do evil and learn to do good" (Isa. 1). This is what normalizing and ritualizing God's ceremonies always does, and they become a burden to both Him and us.

Modern Christianity has truly misinterpreted the winds when it comes to Communion. I hope you will take this opportunity to do as I did and open your eyes to what the Bible really has to say about it.

Leaving the Church to Find Help?

While Communion's power in the church today has suffered, the need for why God instituted it has not. Because the knife has been removed, and yet people still feel the need to employ it in their lives, ever-increasing numbers of the faithful caught up in life's storms pass by churches on their way to recovery programs and Christian therapists every day. They're going to the people they're told will provide an environment conducive to confession, a listening ear to speak in to, and the wisdom and experience necessary to answer their questions. It has now become the practice for churches to refer their emotionally troubled and addicted members to outside professionals because they believe they have lost the ability to fulfill these needs, and this due to the same seeking of comfort and convenience that has led to their flock's dilemma.

> [Author's note: While I will refer to 12-Step recovery programs throughout this book because, in their genesis, they were biblically based and an archetype of Communion, I can no longer recommend them. Truth has been co-opted for the sake of popularity and success, because success means perpetuation of the programs and their funding. We can now see the result of Satan's subversion of 12-Step programs, where Jesus Christ has been removed as the 'higher power.' They now boast a paltry 10%-20% success

rate, with those participating in them on the never-ending Hamster Wheel of recovery that keeps them coming and government subsidies funding. While I will refer to them, I do not endorse such programs any more than I endorse modern observances of Communion.]

Is this what God wants? Are we 'looking for love in all the wrong places?' Does He really want His people to *leave* the church in search of emotional healing? Is God so short-sighted that He failed to provide a biblical, practical healing program for His people within the body? Let me now stand to proclaim loudly and proudly, "NO, for Jehovah Rapha ['The Lord who heals both body and soul'] has provided!" Keeping souls in a constant state of 'healing' is precisely what Communion was ordained to do. He knows we are going to sin and therefore gives us ways to deal with the damage that can do to our souls within the biblical confines of fellowship, not under a doctor/patient model based upon worldly philosophies. We just need to reset the table and reawaken the biblical practice of it.

When properly observed, Communion becomes God's lighthouse in our stormy seas. It brings to the surface all manner of buried sins and suffering, gives us a forum to confront them and neuter their power, attacks the diseases of superficiality and hypocrisy, provides hope for a brighter tomorrow, and brings together fellowships in a bond of unity like no other single ceremony available to us.

As my brave band of young people and I put what God was showing us into practice, lives were transformed before our eyes. Sin addictions that had held people under their control for years were confronted and confessed, brought to light, and their power removed. God revealed Himself through it all and liberated those who blessed Him by honoring the ceremony Jesus still 'earnestly desires to participate in with us' (Luke 22)!

In Remembrance of Grace *and* Truth

Religion takes what is of the Spirit that is never predictable or safe and seeks to make it so. Jesus told Nicodemus the Spirit cannot be structured and Paul said Communion was anything but safe. Like the ceremony, we've also made the One who judges our observance of it predictable and safe by making Him all about grace, love, and forgiveness when that's only part of the story. Biblical Communion is certainly about grace and mercy, but it's about ohhhhh-sooooo much more and that's where we've lost the power of it.

In John 1, Jesus is described as the living Word of God that came to us in the flesh: 'full of grace *and* truth.' Any person who encountered Him came away understanding the abundant comforts of His merciful embrace but, at the same time, had to run the gauntlet of the unnerving challenges presented by His words of teaching, correction, and command.

We've set aside the admonishments and commands from Communion because they're messy, uncomfortable, and inconvenient. But they, too, are a vital part of the rudder God has provided to navigate life's stormy seas. Likewise, we've set aside the truth from the grace in the One who zealously presides over His Passover. The god that presides over today's ceremonies has become what I call The Idol of Grace [discussed fully later on], not the holy and righteous God we are to fear, zealous for justice, and full of grace *and* truth.

What is the 'truth' part of Communion we've conveniently left out that's removed the knife from the place setting? It's that part of Paul's instruction in 1st Corinthians that falls immediately after the words, "Do this in remembrance of Me." He says, "Examine yourself and so eat of the bread and drink of the cup," with dire forewarnings of judgment if this command is circumvented in any way. Because we now ignore the critical aspect of self-examination—the 'knife'—through large group participation with little instruction, a few minutes for reflection and prayer, and no confession and interaction with others in the body that we see those forewarnings now being so widely manifested among the faithful.

When we ignore the balance of grace and truth—when we make Communion about nothing but grace, we strip it of its ability to heal, forcing people to look to worldly counterfeits. The Corinthians made Communion into a social gathering, refusing the command for self-examination, and it led to those dire consequences of physical 'weakness, sickness, and sleep [death]' (1 Cor. 11). They dishonored The Lord's Table with their superficial observances, and it cost them dearly. Sadly, most all church Communions are observed in the same manner, with the same tragic results: *spiritual* weakness, sickness, and sleep in the body of Christ.

Too many churchgoers today 'eat and drink judgment upon themselves' by partaking when they have not taken careful inventory of their spiritual condition and then dealt with it. Even 12-Step ministers and therapists have figured out that love without admonishment and action accomplishes little in the way of true renewal and healing. They've learned it's about honesty, transparency, courage, and actions of repentance leading to healing and grace.

Paul said to the Corinthians [his favorite targets for confrontation, it would seem], "For though I caused you sorrow by my letter, I do not regret it...I now rejoice, not that you were made sorrowful, but that you were made sorrowful to the point of repentance. For you were made sorrowful according to the will of God...For behold what earnestness this very thing, this godly sorrow, has produced in you: what vindication of yourselves, what indignation, what fear, what longing, what zeal, what avenging of wrong" (2 Cor. 7)!

Can you feel the passion of that last sentence? He says repentance leads to 'vindication of oneself' and it is through proper observance of the table we do just that! Paul was unafraid to dispense justice in the form of stern warnings, along with graceful encouragement, because he had personally witnessed the evidence of the fruits of the

Spirit and also the deeds of the flesh taking root in the Corinthians.

If we'd just figure out those our emotionally troubled are flocking to understand the concept of biblical Communion better than most administering it in church, reset the table by reinstituting the balance of grace and truth in our observances, and put the ceremony back into the biblical environment of intimate spiritual family, the hurting would find within the body much of what they are now looking for in places the enemy has successfully infiltrated.

The Spiking Event of Fellowship

Robert Lewis wrote a book about the masculine journeys he and two of his friends embarked upon while raising their sons—a book that any man with a young son should consider a top priority. In *Raising a Modern-Day Knight,* he talks about 'spiking events' that are the culminating, sealing acts of a journey that has taken considerable time, effort, and endurance to complete. They proclaim to the world, "We've been through the valleys, done the work, climbed the mountains, and arrived at the summit!" Lewis relates these journeys to the three primary shots in a volleyball game, the final one being the spike:

> The spike is an aggressive, powerful play. When a player rises to the net and spikes the ball into the other court, he puts an exclamation point on his

team's execution. A good spike finalizes everything his team has worked so hard to accomplish. A ceremony is like the spike. It drives home the point with unmistakable certainty.

God's ultimate gift to the small-group fellowship—*the* ceremony, *the* exclamation point, and the spiking event is Communion! It was the culminating event of Jesus' ministry on earth with His disciples, and the only one of all miracles done and all messages preached of which He said, "I have earnestly desired to partake in this with you" (Luke 22). It is the *spike* that drives home the bond of unity and healing in the fellowship of believers 'with unmistakable certainty.' Jesus' Passover was His disciples' final debriefing and His grand pre-death epitaph summarizing all He had shown and taught them.

If we would but apply the balm of Communion to our emotional and spiritual wounds, we would see the stream of the hurting who now flow out of the church begin to stream back in. All we need to do is arise and shine to a gift that has always been there for us! If you will read on and practice this ceremony with your fellowships, you will discover why Jesus still longs to join us at His Table of Truth and Grace, and through a balance of love and correction, guide our sometimes-frail ships deftly through the storms of life and on to safe harbor.

Chapter II

Whatever Happened to the Passover?

> "I seek the truth...It is only persistence in self-delusion and ignorance which does harm."
> — Marcus Aurelius

Your name is Thaddaeus. You're one of the twelve, and you've been a part of a great adventure with an itinerant preacher for the past three years. While surprises have become a part of life with this Jesus, you've settled into somewhat of a routine. You and the other disciples have spent your time watching everything from the mundane to the miraculous develop along a truly wondrous path. You have been constantly sent out to preach His message and then brought back to His side to discuss your experiences. You've seen the dead raised, the sick healed, water turned to wine, and amazing numbers of people fed to overflowing with one child's basket of food. You've also seen Him play with children, talk quietly with prostitutes and tax collectors, and minister to a wide variety of the most messed-up people no one else would give the time of day.

However, since His recent arrival in Jerusalem, the ride has been as unstable as a moneychanger's table in the temple courts. You and the other disciples cheered in joyous jubilation as He rode triumphantly into the city, but ever since then, this Messiah has seemed on an unrelenting collision course with the religious leaders. The Scribes and Pharisees test Him, peppering Him with trick questions designed to trap Him and further their own purposes. He counters them with a defiance, authority, and wisdom that has left them emotionally unnerved, theologically undressed, and growing more hostile by the day.

During this struggle, it seems Jesus' typically loving mood has changed to outrightly combative, as with every passing moment and every authoritative word coming from His lips, He moves closer and closer to some master plan about which you and the others remain totally clueless. He's been talking about being 'delivered up' and killed, but believing He is the promised Messiah, you and the others can't seem to wrap your heads around His words. Just recently, the tensions boiled over as He was confronted by His robed irritants after healing a blind man. He delivered an angry and stinging rebuke, calling them hypocrites, whitewashed tombs, and a brood of vipers! There had been many such confrontations of late.

Whatever Happened to the Passover? • 15

This One you had come to know as an extraordinary man of peace and love has a face now set like flint toward some daunting gauntlet He knows He must run, but one that nonetheless unnerves and upsets Him. You have this uneasy feeling that what began in triumph is going to end in a no-holds-barred wrestling match for the hearts and minds of the people of Israel and you're going to get caught at ground zero!

The Passover is at hand, and all Jerusalem is in preparation. One of your brothers asks Jesus what He intends to do to celebrate it. In response, He tells two of your fellow disciples to go find a certain man in the city and say to him that He has need of a large room the man owns. They are then to go with him to prepare for the meal. The two leave on their errand, and sometime later, Jesus leads the rest of you to your destination. His mood is somber, and the joy you have come to know this Jesus for has been replaced by a sense of fervent purpose and total dedication to this cause which has captured His thoughts of late.

When all are finally seated, He says something that takes you aback—not that it's earth-shattering in its message, but you've never heard Him say it before of any of the amazing events you have all participated in together. Jesus, with eyes full of intense destiny, says, "I have earnestly desired to eat this Passover with you before I suffer" (Luke 22). Through this incredible journey over the past three years, he has never relayed to you and the others an earnest desire to do something with you. He has just gone and done it. And though He had spoken many times about suffering at the hands of the Jews, somehow you know now it's imminent. The die is about to be cast. You look first to Peter and then to John, thinking surely these two favorites of Jesus would understand what all this means. You find them blankly staring back at you and the others as if to say, "Don't ask us."

Jesus then says something even more unsettling: "Truly, I say to you that one of you will betray Me!" You respond reflexively, "Surely it's not I, this betrayer you speak of?" The others all anxiously ponder the same question, rocked by this revelation. Jesus casts a quick, penetrating stare around the room and continues, "The Son of Man is to go just as it is written of Him, but woe to that man by whom He is betrayed! It would have been good for that man if he had not been born." Uneasiness has now turned to sheer panic as eyes dart fearfully around the room, looking for a culprit. Everyone is wondering who this traitor could possibly be. Then Judas speaks up: "Surely it is not I, Rabbi?" This draws a terse response from Jesus: "You have said it yourself." You don't know why, but Jesus then speaks another mystery to Judas as He dismisses him: "What you do, go and do quickly."

A look of recognition comes over Judas' face and you know that, somehow, he knows exactly what Jesus meant. He leaves the room for some unknown reason, but again, you have a sense that everything happening this night will be a part of the destination Jesus seems intent on pursuing to its ultimate conclusion. You and the others are beginning to see that the end of this story isn't going to be a particularly happy one.

The next act of Jesus doesn't do anything to calm your nerves. He takes a washbowl and begins to wash Peter's feet. Peter, now sharing the concern felt 'round the table, fumbles for the right words to say—anything to soothe the mood of the moment that has become more unnerving with every tick of the clock. So, like the proverbial Bull in the China Shop, Peter ventures into the perilous mood of the evening, carrying on a conversation with Jesus that earns him a rebuke.

It has become clear this is no night for small talk, questioning, or casual banter of any kind. As you have sensed something coming for days, now it becomes dauntingly clear. Whatever this mission Jesus is on, it will be fulfilled and soon, with you and your brothers helplessly along for the ride. Before this night is done, terrible things are going to happen and there is not a thing any of you can do about it. This is a night to listen, watch, and wait for the Master to say or do whatever it is that He seems so intent upon. It will be a night, for better or worse, that none of you will ever forget.

A One-of-a-Kind Event

Jesus didn't say it when He preached the Sermon on the Mount. He didn't say it when He raised Lazarus from the dead, fed the five thousand, turned water into wine, or rode into Jerusalem to thunderous praise. Only of this one event did He say to His disciples, "I have *earnestly desired* to do this with you." The Passover had begun in Israel and, having formed intimate bonds with His hand-selected followers, in His moment of impending distress more than anything else He wanted to celebrate this ceremony with them. Those who heard in parables would have to wait. Those who followed and yet refused to commit fully would have the dining hall door closed to them. This was a night of preparation, both for Jesus and His chosen apprentices who were about to be cast into the ultimate trial by fire. It was an event that would carry on its shoulders both the fate of His disciples, and His new church, forevermore. This was to be a night like no other.

I believe the reason for this desire to partake in His Passover was the life-giving teaching and example He wanted to set before His "ecclesia" as His last act on earth. He was about to hand the baton of His ministry to His church of twelve, for they were about to carry His message to the world without Him. This was to be their final briefing before He kicked them out of the nest in spectacular fashion. As we witness the passion of this moment, the priority Jesus placed on it and that this, His last act on the eve of the most important single event in all of history, we must ask ourselves what has made it the relatively tame, uneventful, and non-threatening ritual it has become today.

So important was this Passover [Communion] that it was one of only two ceremonies ordained by God in the New Testament. The first was baptism: the New Testament equivalent of Old Testament circumcision. Baptism symbolized the public *celebration of new life* in Christ and was, therefore, only done once. The other was Communion, which focuses on the *maintenance of that life* and, therefore, was to be observed regularly. Given proper time, placed in the proper setting, and observed with proper reverence and understanding, Communion keeps our emotional and spiritual readiness tuned up for the minefields of living life as saints in a world full of obstacles.

Again, understanding Jesus' stated mission when He came was restoring 'the lost sheep of the House of Israel' [which He proclaimed to the woman begging for crumbs at His table (Matt. 15) and to His disciples during their commissioning as their priority (Matt. 10)] the maintenance of those sheep once found was equally as important as the initial restoration would be. God always has, and always will, care for His house *first*. He is far more concerned about maintaining a healthy house than going out and bringing more babes into a dysfunctional one. This Passover was the ultimate expression of how Jesus wished His disciples and us to realize that priority, and I believe why it was His last act with them before He went to the cross.

The word *Communion* comes from the Latin *communis* and the Greek *koin,* and it means to have something shared by everyone who participates together in fellowship. The relationship inferred to here infers an intimate partnership exceeding mere association. Yet, our modern-day observances focus on the individual rather than the person as a part of the body, thus removing one of the most critical aspects of them, which is bringing the fellowship to bear on the self-examination process. This is the 'knife' that has been removed in our observances which, like the doctor's scalpel, is designed to cut to bring about healing. Hebrews 4 tells us the Word of God is an active and living sharpened sword, able to cut deeply into our very joints and able to judge the thoughts and intentions of our hearts.

Spoons are for soup and forks for vegetables, but knives are to help us ingest what the Writer of Hebrews calls 'solid food' (Heb. 5). The power of Communion is as much, if not more, found in taking seriously the practical application of the admonishment to examine ourselves as it is the appreciation of grace. Was Jesus 'cut' to bring about our healing? Did He have to suffer the gauntlet before He received the crown? It is no mere coincidence the Passover was His last act before all of that was to happen.

Jesus claimed that whoever ate His flesh and drank His blood would remain in Him and that He would be in them as well (John 6). Communion is an impactful and binding event, much more than a mere symbolic acknowledgment of grace in our lives. His 'body broken' and 'blood poured out,' which spoke of a price to be paid, are to affect us in tangible, lasting ways and those who partake in this food remain in Him, and He in them. The word *remain* is the same word He used in His Passover teachings we find in John 15, where He says we were chosen and appointed to bear fruit that *remains*. It is the word that He also uses when, in that same chapter, He calls us repeatedly to abide [remain] in Him. This is the most complete form of love because it includes an enduring, lasting relationship, and enduring love and faith are what bring us to perfection in the kingdom.

Jesus wants us to be in a continual process of being and bearing fruit that will last a lifetime. Communion exists to regularly mature and perfect what begins at conversion through being a vital element of the ongoing process of sanctification. While it is solely grace that saves us, it is more than just grace that sanctifies us in that we play a role in what becomes a partnership from the moment of conversion on.

Sanctification [Greek: hagiasmos] means to fulfill or complete the process of purification. It is a process that affects a person's heart and lifestyle. Sanctification is the lifelong pursuit of Christ *by* the faithful, enduring follower coupled with the lifelong work of the Holy Spirit *in* that follower—in other words, a partnership. Communion plays a critical role in the sanctification process because it helps us discover what we are, or are not, failing to supply to the partnership.

When the command to examine ourselves is approached with sincere humility and a desire to mature, Communion can and should be unnerving because its 'truth' is designed to reveal struggles that are incumbent in all of us. Whenever we sincerely ask God to search our hearts, try our thoughts, and reveal any sinful ways we may be thinking or living in (Ps. 139), we open a 'Pandora's Box' that is filled with conflict, chaos, and uncertainty. It is anything but safe.

God will bring to remembrance all manner of issues the person who takes proper advantage of His table has shoved into the deep recesses of their minds through rationalization and denial. But *we* must knock, seek, and ask if we want the door to open to us. The Spirit cannot force conviction upon the soul that has become numb to, or disinterested in, His promptings. The healing made available to us through Communion must begin with this unnerving spotlight shown into our darkness if we want to truly experience the benefits of His grace there.

The Writer of Hebrews would call this accepting the discipline that, when embraced and endured, would bring about 'the peaceful fruit of righteousness' (Heb. 12), but in the comforts of America we have come to want to go straight to dessert rather than beginning with the meat and vegetables. A diet of nothing but sweets typically leads to an upset stomach, sort of like the one Jesus experienced when observing the fruit of the Laodiceans (Rev. 3). They also consumed a steady diet of the deserts of wealth, comfort, and power that have become the norm here, and they made the mistake of thinking because they were 'rich and in need of nothing' in the world all was well in the kingdom.

Reaping Superficiality

What does 'remembering' the grace without the truth yield in our modern observances? Tina Griego, a columnist for the Denver Post, wrote the following review shortly after she had viewed the movie *The Passion of the Christ*:

> It is a gauntlet thrown. A provocation...It demands we confront not just what we believe, but whether our lives offer testimony to those beliefs...It was a movie I very much wanted to see and very much didn't...I knew it would make me uncomfortable, because when it comes to matters of God and religion, I am both un-reconciled and full of longing. It is an ancient ache.

I believe many in the church today feel that 'ancient ache' because they know they are disconnected when it comes to who they are compared to what the Bible says they should be. They desire to know Jesus in a more real way—a way that leads them to think and act more like the believers they read about in those hallowed pages. They see the example Jesus set and hear His words that command them to look increasingly more like Him, but they're not getting there. Words like the ones from John, "The one who says he abides in Him ought himself to walk in the same manner as He walked" (1 John 2), bring about that ancient ache. This disconnect is the definition of *superficiality*.

We all stumble from time to time in our attempts to follow Jesus. It is not that we err that matters as much as it is in how we handle those transgressions when they occur, resulting in how we live life. If left unattended, those temporary slip-ups will eventually become sin patterns that define us as the numbness to them grows. This is followed by a feeling of disconnection from God and the fellowship.

Paul says, "Are we to continue in sin so that grace may increase? May it never be! How shall we who died to sin still live in it" (Rom. 6)? There is a line of persistent disobedience grace will not cross. If we persist in disobedient thoughts and lifestyles, we will ultimately draw that line and it will result in disconnection.

Communion observed properly gently forces participants to listen to God and then deal with the sin that has made the separation and cut them off from the only voice that truly matters. It properly assaults superficiality because it demands we 'confront not only our beliefs but whether our lives support those beliefs.' And that is a good thing because we must face our temporary shortcomings before they snowball into destructive patterns. We must come under the penetrating light of God's convictions and the confrontation of the fellowship at the table, and discover where we have become unreconciled with both.

One tried and tested way to discern the existence of superficiality is simply to review schedules and financial expenditures. How people spend their time and money is many times the truest test of what's going on in their hearts. Do our schedules regularly include time with God, time in fellowship, and time in kingdom pursuits? Would they reveal who in our lives we are evangelizing, discipling, or serving in the love of Christ? Are there any entries in our calendars to engage in regular fellowship beyond church walls? Are there times to be Good Samaritans to the needy outside the church, or to do some talking or listening over a cup of coffee with a group of brothers and sisters or a hurting friend? If the answer to these questions contradicts who we claim to be, superficiality exists.

Then there's the checkbook, for where our earthly treasure is, there our hearts also are (Matt. 6). In affluent societies like ours, the demand that we 'keep up with the Jones's" takes the idea of provision far beyond any recognition of biblical constraints. Claiming to be Christian while spending 50-60 hours per week working for earthly gain, and yet having no time for family or tilling the fields for the kingdom of heaven on earth, is sin and the definition of superficiality.

Are participants giving regularly to something other than their church or exceeding the typical 10% tithe? Do they ever give to anyone without demanding a tax deduction for themselves? Do they spend all the extra funds they have on their own desires? Do their credit card and mortgage balances reveal they are living beyond their means and becoming enslaved to debt to maintain lifestyles they really can't afford? These questions indicate whether they trust in their money or in God.

People can easily deceive themselves into thinking they are putting God first, but it's hard to argue with the schedule and checkbook.

Isaiah: A Warning and a Promise

In Isaiah 1, we find what Paul would refer to as a passage that reveals 'both the kindness and severity of God' (Rom. 11). It is a fitting analogy to what we see happening today with our religious Communion rituals. God declares, "Wounds and bruises and putrefying sores, they have not been closed, bound up, or soothed with ointment...Hear the word of the Lord...Give ear to the instruction of your God...' What are your multiplied sacrifices to Me? I have had enough of burnt offerings of rams and the fat of fed cattle...When you come to appear before Me who requires of you this trampling of My courts? Bring your worthless offerings no longer...I cannot endure iniquity and the solemn assembly...Your festivals and feasts have become a burden to Me and I am weary of bearing them. So when you spread out your hands in prayer, I will hide My eyes from you. Yes, even though you multiply prayers I will not listen..."

    Hard words, yes, but they were necessary to wake up His sleeping people who had forsaken Him and forgotten the reasons for His ordained ceremonies. If we compare His warnings then to the weakness, sickness, and sleep Paul had witnessed in those who had been stricken by the very same curses we see here, and for similar reasons, can we say these 'Christians' were any different? They came repeatedly into the most solemn assembly of all and sullied it with their superficial, hypocritical worship. Were they not failing to 'examine themselves' and so come before a holy God in their ceremonies? Were they not being judged—'stricken over and over again' every time they did? Were they wondering why it seemed God wasn't hearing their prayers? Do we not, by failing to employ the knife in our solemn assemblies, incur repeatedly the same kind of judgements? Paul warned those who failed to properly examine themselves would be 'eating and drinking in judgement.' The polls seem to say that's exactly what's going on.

Ah, but then as always Jehovah remembers His covenant, and that He is the God of reconciliation and salvation, and continues, "Wash yourselves and make yourselves clean. Remove the evil of your deeds from My sight. Cease to do evil, learn to do good, seek justice, reprove the ruthless, defend the orphan and plead for the widow. 'Come now and let us reason together' says the Lord. Though your sins are as scarlet they will be as white as snow. Though they are red like crimson they will be like wool. If you consent and obey, you will eat the best of the land." What I will refer to as the reset table is *the place* for this washing, repenting, and 'reasoning together' with God! It is here we come to have our sins turned from scarlet to bright white and our hard hearts softened like wool, but not without the knife that must cut deeply to do its work. Communion presents the opportunity to let Him examine us, and for us to examine ourselves within the body of Christ, and through all that 'reasoning together' the opportunity to be cleansed and healed!

God said that a mark of false teachers would be the proclamation of peace when there was no peace. Communion is anything but a message of peace without the required work of repentance we have made it today. No. 'It is a gauntlet thrown, a provocation'—a wild and wooly, dangerous, and piercing look into the battle that rages within our souls as children of God battling the flesh and a fallen world! While it will eventually bring about the peaceful fruit of righteousness, to make it to that point initially demands that some chaos and that 'discipline that seems sorrowful' be involved.

If we 'trample the courts' of self-examination, we then embrace a false peace that leads us into thinking wrong conduct is acceptable. When we take the gift meant to undo sinful patterns and allow it to *excuse* us of them instead, the gift transforms from ally to enemy and from being a joy to God to 'a burden He tires of enduring.' Instead of seeking God's help in facing our demons, deal with them, and be healed, we make Communion a vehicle that allows us to feel forgiven when we are not, letting us continue in sin while still thinking everything is good. This *always* renders us people who are unable to connect what we believe with how we live.

No Fear!

Like any change in the status quo, facing the gauntlets of a Communion service that performs as intended will provide some initial discomfort and yield resistance. Even those willing to try may find it difficult to participate fully at first. Yet, if we'll just press on, a most wonderful adventure awaits us! It will be many things, but tepid, lukewarm, and superficial will not be among them.

At the table, I have seen lives transformed, relationships restored, lost souls won for Christ, and hard, dry pottery changed into soft, moldable clay spinning gladly upon the Potter's wheel! I have personally witnessed the reawakening of many self-deceived and oppressed souls, shallow relationships given new substance, and superficial Sunday gatherers transformed into disciples with a new depth of faith and purpose. With that comes the power to act boldly upon the Spirit's convictions, putting sinful practices behind us so that healing might begin.

Communion is the single-most healing proceeding anyone who will fully engage can be involved in. It is God's supreme gift—*the spike*—given specifically for His people's emotional and spiritual maintenance—transforming ancient aches into current healing. Communion is a masterfully devised ceremony that moves us decisively away from the curse of superficiality and toward a new reality with both God and the fellowship.

When placed within Communion's environment, it is amazing to see how quickly formerly unreceptive people respond to the surgical work of the Holy Spirit. Believers and unbelievers alike are irresistibly attracted to the perfect balance of discipline and grace they all crave. People invite friends because once understood and experienced, the table comes to be viewed with excitement and anticipation. Former participants I had not seen for years returned from out of town asking, "Are you still doing that Communion thing? When's the next one?" Is this the way the members of your church feel about The Lord's Supper? Is it the way you feel about it?

This work is a guide to what I believe God instituted to be our consistent and deeply revealing wake-up call—our recovery program from practiced sin and addictions that can lead to all manner of emotional and spiritual dysfunction. This is a ceremony ordained to remind us of our continual need to examine ourselves and face truthfully our standing before Him in light of the piercing truths of His Word. It is a regular gauntlet thrown down to do something concrete about the cover-ups He will always reveal whenever we act in obedience to His Word.

This wonderful opportunity—this ultimate weapon we have been given to fight the cursed sleep that has made our spiritual eyes heavy—this blessed reminder of the reality of the healing power of repentance, confession, prayer, and action isn't some new revelation. Rather, it is an ancient ceremony that has lost something in an American culture that seeks worldly comfort instead of spiritual truth and a church that has come to look far too much like it. I close this chapter with a true story of a young man brought from hypocrisy and deception to the truth via one biblically observed Communion ceremony.

Jeremy [all names fictitious] sporadically attended our Young Life small group and then graduated from high school. I lost track of him until he suddenly reappeared in my life some fifteen years later. In High School this young man lived a relatively worldly life. He was unwilling to commit himself fully to Christ, being far more interested in perfecting his rock-n-roll guitar skills. However, one of the last things he did with us before leaving for college was to attend one of our Communion services.

When we once again met those many years later, he was touring the country, leading fellowships in worship songs he had written. He now used those considerable musical gifts to spread the Gospel and had become a dedicated disciple of Jesus. I asked him about the miraculous turnaround I saw in his life, and what it was that sparked the commitment I now saw. He said simply, "That Communion service I attended in your group before I left for college exposed me as the Christian poser I was. It made me think."

Here was a young man who had come from darkness to light and from preaching a message of darkness, immorality, and hopelessness to one of life, hope, love, and the kingdom—a 'new creature in Christ' who had, and would continue to, change lives with the gospel! It had all been made possible through one simple ceremony that has always been there for us—one ordained to expose the posers we all can become, 'make us think,' and transform us into kingdom citizens.

So, to answer the question, "Whatever happened to the Passover?" It's there, we've simply lost the biblical understanding of its purpose and how to release its power. As Ms. Hale quoted, now we can 'come and find the things not lost to us, but that we lost.' It's time for us to stop hiding from it" and to rediscover and reawaken it. In our quest for a comfortable faith, we've lost the meaning of that most important admonishment to examine ourselves as a *prerequisite* for partaking. It's been replaced by a 'private, token, and not terribly upsetting look at our unreconciled issues which has created that ancient ache.'

In our search to find what happened to the biblical Passover, we will examine four areas in Scripture:

- The Passover and Exodus of the Jews.
- The Gospel accounts of Christ's last supper with His disciples in Matthew 26, Mark 14, Luke 22, and John 13-17.
- The church of Pentecost in Acts 2.
- Paul's Communion instructions in 1st Corinthians 11.

In the consistent message of these teachings, we will discover an event full of power and the conviction of the Holy Spirit that has been covered up but still has a heartbeat. We will reawaken a ceremony that can take us back in time to the church of Pentecost and the indelible mark of intimate fellowship it fostered in all who partook of its wonders. As did John, I can testify, "Truly, truly, I say to you, 'I speak that which I know and bear witness of that which I have seen'" (John 3). I have witnessed the fruit of 'doing this in remembrance of *all of Him*' and know these words to be true.

So, join me if you will in a hopefully eye-opening walk through the incredible riches God has awaiting in an intimate Passover/Communion experience. Understand why Jesus desired so fervently to partake in it with His disciples as He now does with you. Rejoice in the love that waits for you there in abundance. But also, be prepared to fully embrace Christ's challenging admonishments you will encounter, which will lead to the boundless benefits from the healing power of partaking in the table God established and is no-longer pass(ed)over!

Chapter III

To Unbelievers and Believers

> Different people need different sorts of
> communication for it to have the same effect.
> — Tobias Lutke

Any properly reset table must address to whom it is open and why. Jesus' Passover was available only to His disciples, and an objective examination of Paul's teachings in 1st Corinthians 11 reveals an exclusivity in participation as well. Verses 23-26 could be called the admonitions for the unbeliever, and verses 27-32 those for the believer.

As to the former, Paul warns, "The Lord Jesus...said, 'Do this, as often as you drink it, in remembrance of Me. For as often as you eat this bread and drink the cup, you proclaim the Lord's death until He comes" (vs. 23-26). *Proclaim* here [Greek: kataggello] is not a passive word. It means affirmatively declaring something—to preach or to teach it with conviction. When we take Communion, we *affirmatively* proclaim to all participants gathered, along with any who may be looking on, that we are believers dedicated to proclaiming with our words, and modeling with our lives, Jesus Christ and His kingdom for the two are inseparable.

Without acceptance of the work Jesus accomplished on the cross, which is represented by the body broken and the blood poured out, the rest of the gospel becomes irrelevant because it was this act that paved the way to repentance for sin, salvation, and entrance into the kingdom of heaven on earth. Without understanding and embracing that, and then believing in and attesting to the presence of the Holy Spirit in one's life it made possible, how could anyone possibly 'proclaim' the Lord's death? Therefore, it is a simple matter to understand that those who do not believe in the crucified, resurrected Christ have no place at His Holy Table.

Accepting that cautioning any unbelieving onlookers to abstain is an act of love rather than judgment, they should, by all means, be encouraged to stay and observe. They should feel free to ask questions while at the same time respecting the seriousness and spirit of the proceedings. I have seen souls won to Christ by witnessing biblical Communion in action because, when properly observed, there exists no better place to witness true Christian community that Jesus said He wanted to be known by.

Twice in John 17 [the 'High Priestly Prayer'] Jesus asks the Father to make his disciples one in the unity of the fellowship 'so that the world may know the Father sent

Him.' He also said the world would know we were His disciples by the 'love we had for *one another*' (John 13). Jesus' people gathered together in unity and love makes the Communion setting the best possible place for the lost to see real and honest fellowship they may have never witnessed in religious gatherings before.

While it would not be wise to invite a number of unbelievers to the ceremony, we need to encourage those who do come to stay and keep an open mind as to what the Holy Spirit may want us to pass on. At the same time, we need to lovingly admonish them that they cannot partake of the elements until they give their lives to, and can then *proclaim*, the One who provided the body and blood.

The Message to Believers

The far more important, and more complicated, message is to believers. Is it open to anyone who has 'prayed the prayer' as we have made it today? The purpose of this book is to say, "No." Yes, communion gives us great reassurance of the love and forgiveness available to us in Paul's initial passages. The believer can realize anew every time they come it is in Christ and His sacrifice 'so new every morning' (Lam. 3) they can be renewed there.

Ah, but now the unbeliever's warning and the believer's reassurance of verses 23-26 take a turn that has become too discomforting to be observed in the traditional church. Here Paul begins cautioning the believer, "Therefore whoever eats the bread or drinks the cup of the Lord in an unworthy manner shall be guilty of the body and blood of the Lord. But let a man examine himself, and so let him eat of the bread and drink of the cup. For he who eats and drinks, eats and drinks judgment to himself if he does not judge the body rightly. For this reason, many among you are weak and sick, and a number sleep" (vs. 27-30).

Two points here confirm that this portion of the Communion instruction specifically targets believers. The first is Paul's use of the word *sleep*. Matthew 27 and John 11 contain this same word [Greek: koimesis], which means to lie down and sleep. It is used only in reference to the physical passing of the flesh of believers. However, there is a double meaning here. Jesus said if we believed in Him, though our bodies would suffer decay and cease to function, our souls and spirits would never die (John 11). But the Bible also speaks of physical and eternal death of those who perish outside the faith. Therefore, there is the need for two separate words to describe death: one that refers to the passing of the flesh only of believers and one that refers to the death—body and soul—of all others.

When the Bible refers to the cessation of life of an unbeliever, the word used is *nekros* [Greek: death]. If Paul were addressing unbelievers, as he is in verses 23-26, this word would be *nekros* and not *koimesis*. By saying many in Corinth had fallen asleep as a result of their superficial observances of the Lord's Table, Paul is saying that they had actually died in the flesh. This is not so hard to believe as it was a time in the history of Christ's church when people physically and suddenly perished because of sin [see the story of Annas and Sapphira in Acts 5].

Hypocrisy wasn't something to toy with then as we do today. While we see little judgment of this sort occurring in our times, once again I ask, do we not find many in the church who are spiritually weak, sick, and asleep? According to all the polls of evangelized churchgoers taken over the past decades, over 90% live in this precise condition. If we look upon it with spiritual eyes, the power of the God who watches over His table is still very, very real.

The second indication that Paul is targeting the saved in this segment of his instruction revolves around the issue of internal judgment by the fellowship. Paul says that if we judged *ourselves* rightly, we would not be judged. But *when* we are judged, we are disciplined by the Lord, so we won't be condemned along with the world (vs. 31-32). In another instruction to the Corinthians, Paul asks, "For what have I to do with judging outsiders? Do you not judge those who are *within* the church? But those who are outside God judges" (1 Cor. 5). Paul clearly distinguishes between those we in the church should judge and those we should not. He says that we have nothing to do with judging outsiders [unbelievers] but then asks the Corinthians why they refuse to judge themselves?

The clear message is that believers alone belong because here is where righteous judgement: God judging the fellowship and the fellowship judging itself, is to occur. There is one judgment for the believer and another judgment for the unbeliever. God judges both, but we play a part in the latter by judging ourselves as individuals and as a body.

Being Righteously Judgmental

Judgment has become a four-letter word amongst the faithful today. But when you think about it, we enter into judgment every day of our lives. Do we, or our children, associate with this person or that? Is an investment we are about to make going to lead to profit or loss? Is what we are about to do right or wrong? Will any of the many decisions we make from moment to moment lead us off track or keep us on God's path? The word *judge* [Greek diakrino] means simply to discern, and wise people use it to protect themselves, others, and their circumstances on a regular basis.

Inasmuch as Paul delivers such a clear warning for those who believe in Christ to be righteously judgmental among their own members, how does that fit into the Communion environment? Given the fact that the self-deceived believer will often play the 'You're-judging-me' card as a first line of defense, we need to know how to respond with an answer that overcomes their argument and leads them back to repentance and the truth.

Jesus provided the perfect response to this type of deflection in John 12 when He said, "He who rejects Me and does not receive My sayings has one who judges him. The word I spoke is what will judge him at the last day."

God also declared through Zechariah, "These are the things which you should do: speak the truth to one another, and judge with truth and judgment for peace in your gates" (Zech. 8). When we admonish one another in a spirit of Christ's love, and with biblical truth on our side, we must refuse to back down when accused of being judgmental. Our words aren't judging the unrepentant, be they sinner or saint, but rather the words of God Himself are doing the convicting and boldly speaking the truth is the only loving thing to do to make it heard.

In John 16, Jesus foretold of the Holy Spirit who would come 'convicting the world concerning sin and righteousness and judgment.' That doesn't stop with the unbeliever. It is *always* the right thing to do to admonish a self-deceived brother or sister with the truth of God's Word, in a spirit of love and with the goal of restoration. Jesus *always* did so with His people, His mission being to the lost sheep of His Father's House. You do not excuse a lost sheep, nor do you coddle it, for if you do it will continue to wander from the flock and be vulnerable to attack by predators. Shepherds would go so far as to break the legs of sheep who constantly wandered from the flock for their own good. 'Tis better to suffer a broken leg than to become an easy meal for a prowling lion. The trick is to do it at the right place and time, and God has provided both in the Communion ceremony.

Without righteous judgment [discernment] we will never find true healing within the church. The Word of God is designed to pierce through the denials and rationalizations of the self-deceived. Speaking it will take the focus off of you, where the enemy is desperately trying to keep it so he can keep his captives from facing it in themselves. Letting them know their issues are between God and them, and not you and them, will place that focus on the One with whom they cannot argue and who has the power to invade their twilight zones of self-illusion. It will also establish you as a true friend who is there to help them through it.

Peter said it was time for judgment to *begin* with the household of God (1 Pet. 4) and we are to approach this process as 'diligent workmen who do not need to be ashamed because we handle the truth accurately' (2 Tim. 2). Admonishing those living in illusions with the Word is simply not an option if we truly love people. Louis Berkhof, in his book *Systematic Theology*, relates the need for the church to police herself when it comes to allowing the unrepentant at the table:

> And if the unbelief and ungodliness [of the unrepentant] becomes evident, the church will have to exclude them [from Communion] by the proper administration of church discipline. The holiness of the church and of the sacrament must be safeguarded [words in parenthesis mine].

Throughout history, God has provided prophets who have proclaimed loudly and single-mindedly, "Turn around, repent, and amend your ways or the judgment of Him who is faithful and true is coming upon you!" It's our choice: judge ourselves within the fellowship or have it brought down upon us from above.

If we would but utilize the gift of Communion to judge ourselves regularly within the righteous confines of intimate fellowship, and this through objective individual and corporate self-examination, we wouldn't have to face the more costly option of dealing with the conviction David describes in Psalm 32. It is always true that consequences are fewer and less severe when we act upon small transgressions before they turn into larger, protracted ones.

If those shepherding The Lord's Table will but boldly teach and then enforce the warnings to both believers and unbelievers, molehills will stop becoming mountains and regular maintenance will replace crisis management when lives have begun to fall apart. The burdens of major surgery and chemo will be replaced by the much lighter yoke of regular check-ups to remove the lumps before they become cancerous.

The unbelievers' instruction here is simple. They don't need to discern where deception, cover-up, and superficiality may exist. They only need to think about whether or not to place their faith in Jesus Christ. For believers, the self-examination process can be much more involved, difficult, and chaotic. That is why we come together in this divinely inspired ceremony held in an environment of established fellowship with those we trust, custom-tailored to help us confront the scrutiny and truth of God's dismantling convictions and then act upon them.

Chapter IV

Recognizing Sin

> "Something within us must die, and we must be the executioners. We are not to let it live while we try to behave better."
> — Dr. Larry Crabb

I once attended an Episcopal Easter Sunday service in the desert of California, where my wife and I often enjoyed our spring vacation with family. I remember being struck by the absolute beauty of this sanctuary: towering, vaulted ash-paneled ceilings, expansive glazing everywhere looking out to crystal blue desert skies, palm trees, and ornate flower gardens there in the Coxiella Valley. There was nary a cloud in the sky, a diverse symphony of birds was singing, and the ever-present smell of orange blossoms filled the air. But I came to find out the beauty was only skin deep.

Shortly after we were seated, I noticed two middle-aged men who walked down the aisle and sat in the front row.

They stood out in the crowd because they wore matching bright white-and-black cowboy shirts, blue jeans, and cowboy hats and boots—attire that was hardly the order of the day given the prevailing climate and the mostly-elderly membership. Someone beside me noticed my interest in them and exclaimed, "Those two are really something. They ride up every Sunday on their Harleys and always sit in the same spot in the front row. They're very devoted to the church...and they're gay."

Not long after the service began Communion was served, Paul's instructions ended with 'Do this in remembrance of Me,' no warnings at all were given, and everyone in a church of several hundred [save me and one other couple] got up and went forward. And yes, the two gay motorcycle jockeys were the first to joyously partake from the very hand of the proud, smiling Anglican priest.

I was at once saddened by the thought of two men being allowed to think God blessed their sinful lifestyles, but even more sickened by the thought of the false shepherd who administered over such a desecration of the Holy Sacraments—the very ceremony God gave to confront such lifestyles used rather to enable and enforce them! Mind you, homosexuality is no different than the myriad conditions under which people unworthily partake every day.

Homosexuality is, however, a very good example of the type of sinful conduct that one *practices* that will 'leaven' every part of life. Like any other sin, it can be repented of, and, like any other sin, it must be confronted by the church rather than blessed by it. By ignoring the Lord's admonishments in our Communion ceremonies, cover-ups are allowed to survive, thereby consigning those participating unworthily to their sin. The 'severe rebuke' from both God and a brother or sister in Christ has a *compassionate* goal, and that is to call us back from the brink. That is why Dietrich Bonhoeffer said, "Nothing can be more compassionate than the severe rebuke that calls a brother back from the path of sin."

The 'something that must die' Crabb speaks of at any ceremony concerned with purity is the influence of the flesh. It is the tenaciousness of our enemy and our sinful nature that led Jesus to command us to 'deny ourselves and take up our crosses *daily*' (Luke 9). Satan's own self-deceptive nature dictates that he will never, this side of his final judgment, believe that he can possibly lose this fight. Therefore, no matter how many times we throttle him, he will get right back up and keep on coming at us through our flesh.

It, and he, are not to be understood or allowed to succeed but rather to be decisively battled with every weapon available, and we must take a proactive role in the execution! It is not a battle God will take on for us alone, but one in which He will gladly join as we take up His full armor and go forth in obedience and enduring faith.

While it may sound risky to seek a deeper revelation of our sinful nature, the beginning of a cure for any disease is found in accurate discernment of the problem. People asked to confront sin who have been unaccustomed to it are often confused because the very nature of Laodicean superficiality and self-deception is to think they don't have a problem when, in fact, they do.

Many of us have experienced the 'thorn-in-the-flesh' kind of sin we struggle with daily and yet oftentimes seem powerless to do anything about. I struggled with mine for over 40 years. The enemy is constantly attempting to blind us to our shortcomings, especially those that haunt us regularly, so we become numb and just go along to get along. Because he understood the nature of the beast we face, Peter said, "I will always be ready to remind you of these things, even though you already know them and have been established in the truth which is present with you. I consider it right, as long as I am in this earthly dwelling, to stir you up by way of reminder" (2 Pet. 1).

Peter is saying no matter where our station is with God and no matter how long we have been with Him or what we have come to know—no matter how mature we may be or how many years we have spent following Him, we cannot presume there is no work to be done concerning purity and holiness. Why? Because he, like Paul in Romans 7, knew of the life-long struggle with his unwanted houseguest, the flesh. Applying this to Communion we need to acknowledge we can never—ever—come to the table presuming all is good and we don't need to stop and take that self-exam. *We need to be just as vigilant in staying alert as our enemy is in trying to put us to sleep.*

When participants' minds are 'stirred up' by faithful administrators of the table so their eyes can be reopened to specific areas of sin in their lives, they will be better able to deal with them. While we could fill volumes with every sin under the sun, a good starting point for examining some basics of self-deception and stalled spiritual growth can be found in examining Satan's favorite lie and God's first commandment.

The Foundations of Sin

Satan's favorite lie is contained in the first book of the Bible and also in one of the last. This demonstrates the fact that, throughout time, it has never changed. Perhaps this is because it has always worked so well. The adage, "If it isn't broken, don't fix it" would seem to apply. Comparing Genesis 3:6 and 1st John 2:16, we find that the master-deceiver has always fed upon 'the lust of the flesh [the fruit good for food], the lust of the eyes [a delight to the eyes] and the boastful pride of life [desirability to make one wise].' From these arise a polluted spring from which most other areas of subsequent sin sprout:

- Wrong priorities [lust of the flesh]: The Great Commandment (Matthew 10:37-39, and Colossians 1:16-18) reveals the absolute truth that Jesus Christ needs to be number one in our lives. Any possessions or desires placed above knowing Him, and He us, become idols with which God says He will not share His throne. Some typical idols would be jobs, material possessions, addictions. coveting what others have, or any other thing or position that may be the primary focus of one's desires, most of which spring from the desires of our flesh.

- Spirit of unforgiveness [boastful pride of life]: 2 Corinthians 2:10-11, Mark 11:25-26, and Colossians 3:13 deal with refusal to forgive anyone of *any* transgression. Such harbored resentment, sadly rearing its ugly head so often today within the dysfunction of our families, finds its genesis in pride and stands flatly in opposition to Jesus' command to love those who mistreat and abuse us (Matt. 5). The Lord says He will refuse His forgiveness to anyone who likewise refuses to forgive their brothers and sisters (Matt. 18). Unforgiveness stops our sanctification dead in its tracks until it is dealt with. To the table, of all places, we need to come forgiving *and* forgiven to the extent we have the power to do so.

- Lust of the flesh and of the eyes: Matthew 5:27-28 and 1st Corinthians 6:18 reveal lust is the one sin that Paul tells us to *flee* from. It is the one that will win every time unless we remove its catalysts entirely from our lives and our minds. This transgression, a sin which we are not to even attempt to stand toe-to-toe against, is absolutely pervasive in its enslavement of believers today. Thanks to the internet, pornography's overwhelming availability is making it a growing problem for people of all ages and sexes in the church.

Lust is the one that dismantled David's family: the man who 'had a heart after God's own.' It also undid Solomon, 'the wisest man who ever lived.' Even the purest of heart and the most knowledgeable in the Scriptures are no match for this temptation if they don't turn tail and run for their lives!

- Hard-heartedness [the boastful pride of life]: John 9:39-41, Romans 2:4-5, and Numbers 15:30-31 reveal the dangers of a hard heart. This one awaits to snare even the mature child of God because the good we do for Him and the knowledge we accumulate of Him can be such fertile soil for its growth. A religious spirit that supplants true faith through a belief we become somehow better than those we perceive don't know, or follow Him as closely as we do, is the perfect culture to grow this sin.

Paul warned that 'knowledge would puff us up' and that if any of us thought we knew anything 'we didn't yet know as we ought to know' (1 Cor. 8). This was the sin of the Pharisees, who were the only ones Jesus regularly crossed swords with. Their religious pride was the reason they refused to be taught anything by Him, even though they should have been the first to have recognized Him. Hard-heartedness working through the pride of accumulated knowledge and accomplishment is a disease that can put the most tenured believers on the thinnest of ice with our God, and it is the cornerstone of a religious spirit.

- Love of the world: Paul said the first step of a transformational mind-renewal process was to 'no longer be conformed to this world' (Rom. 12). John said, "Do not love the world nor the things in the world. If anyone loves the world, the love of the Father is not in him" (1 John 2). I have already discussed the issue of money, so suffice it to say if participants' lives look more like the worldly than the godly, there is work to be done so that they may get back into an abiding relationship with Jesus.

Again, I could go on and on, but these are some of the basics that need to be discussed to "stir people up by way of reminder' because Satan attempts to put people to sleep by way of forgetting through denial, cover-up, and rationalization. Regular self-exams provide for us a critical discerning of the Devil and his plots through inviting the Spirit to bless the reasons for Communion.

Living in Sin

Paul told us to *run* from immorality and James instructed us to submit to God and to resist the Devil (James 4). Sinning is one thing but living a sinful lifestyle is another. Breaking free from the strongholds of sin Satan has been able to secure in our lives means dealing with both our spiritual condition and our lifestyle, for they cannot be segregated. Jesus said the tree is known by its fruit (Luke 6), and the tree of our spiritual condition cannot help but be known by the fruit manifested in our lifestyles.

The popular term for sinful lifestyles is 'living in sin,' which classically refers to two believers living together out of wedlock. It is living in sin because those involved could repent every moment of every day, and yet the very next second, they are back to living in the sinful state they are constantly immersed in. This condition is by no means limited to living out of wedlock. It applies to any consistent unbiblical practice. Repenting from such lifestyles is not true repentance, because if it were, not only words of sorrow would be offered but 'deeds appropriate to repentance' (Acts 26) as well, resulting in breaking off the relationship. The chances of getting freed of sinful spiritual conditions do not exist where lifestyle settings never change.

I remember a famous Christian basketball star in Denver who later went on to coach the Nuggets. He had temper and language issues he admitted to, even as he was out speaking and teaching at Christian functions when his schedule permitted. His shortcomings would be on display for all to see as he ranted, raved, and threw around expletives like so much dust in the wind before thousands watching the games he coached. He truly loved basketball and loved coaching, but it put him in a position where his physical environment fed the fires of a sinful spiritual condition and made him look to the eyes of all watching like the world's biggest hypocrite. He finally stepped down when one of his tirades with a heckling fan became racial in nature, and the media climbed all over it.

The Bible calls us to forsake our worldly circumstances and to follow Jesus. How difficult would it have been for Matthew to continue as a tax collector for Rome and yet tell people he was a disciple of Christ? How difficult would it have been for Paul to continue dragging Christians from their churches and homes to punish or even kill them and be known as the great apostle he became? Their former conduct could never have continued because the Spirit who transforms all He truly indwells did not allow it.

A great difference exists between doing all possible to follow God, while occasionally stumbling, and making a practice of stumbling while occasionally following God. Our lifestyles give a clear indication of which of those two we embrace. If people trapped in compromising spiritual or physical environments are willing to take the often drastic, self-sacrificing steps to extricate themselves they are to be encouraged, applauded, and welcomed on board, for they have made a paradigm shift from 'living as sinners,' to living as repentant saints!

Jesus Always Does His Part

Jesus is not to be blamed when believers fail to mature in their faith through becoming trapped in destructive sin patterns for the door to repentance, leading to His renewed presence, is always open. Once the sin is recognized and acknowledged, He can and will jump in and get those hands that were nailed to the cross dirty! Peter stresses we 'have been given *everything* concerning life and godliness' (2 Pet.1). Jesus is the 'author *and* perfecter of our faith' and is always proactive in our experience. He has done His part to first forgive sin and then ensure that everything we need to become mature is fully available to us through the indwelling power of the Holy Spirit. As the Father of His prodigals, He will always come running when we recognize our transgressions, turn from them, and open the door to reconciliation. The Good Shepherd will always go before His obedient children as they repent *from* the past and *to* the future He always has waiting in the wings.

We are the ones who give Satan footholds to exert power over us, and inasmuch as sin is present in our flesh, he will always find places and ways to attack if we leave them open. As a deliverance minister, I have learned that demonic oppression must begin with us giving 'permissions' to the demons to come in. While there are instances where they come in through circumstances we have no control over [abuse in the womb, times when we are anesthetized, generational curses, etc.], by far the most common permission points are granted to them by us through our thoughts, our words, and our actions. Where they have no permission, they cannot enter.

The footholds we give to the flesh must be, as Dr. Crabb recommends, "Grabbed by the neck and throttled, and throttled again every time they show up." And they will show up. But Jesus stands ready to do His part also, every time and without fail, and "Greater is He who is in us than he who is in the world" (1 John 4). His Spirit will convict us, empower us to confess, forgive us, clean us up, set us back on our feet, and cheer us on every time we take advantage of the many tools He has given us.

The Goal? Deliverance!

Where addictions and other ongoing sin patterns are concerned, I would recommend an excellent tool to be considered is deliverance, a concept largely misunderstood in the church. This is unfortunate because many who could benefit from it shy away. I ran on what I came to call the Hamster Wheel of discipline and accountability for decades, as I fought lusting after flesh. It wasn't until a good friend kicked a few nasty demons out of my life—agents of Satan I had no idea were even there, that I was finally set free! And make no mistake, the goal of God is always deliverance, not endless helpings of discipline and accountability.

In my battle, I read books and regularly involved myself in Christian 12-Step knockoffs. I truly believed it was all that was available to me to survive without going totally off the rails. How embarrassing: living day after day after day with the guilt and shame of the ongoing fight against my sinful thoughts and the actions they led to. Some days I would win and some I would lose, but the temptation was *always* there from the moment I awoke to the time I went to sleep. Even though I realized Satan's power of denial and was always willing to confess and come under accountability, the fight persisted.

But then, as I was sitting in one of those groups where everyone was proud to be 'recovering addicts,' the Lord began to show me two things: first, every time I declared my sinful condition to these groups, I was just reinforcing my association with it. I was saying, as much to me as to others, "I'm a hopeless sinner, but I'm sure working on my recovery!" He asked me questions like, "Did I come to make you a recovered sinner or a saint? Am I not the God of deliverance? Do you believe you are a new creature, the old things passed away and all things becoming new (2 Cor. 5)? Have I not called you a Royal Priest and did I not come to bring you joy instead of burden? Why exactly did my Son die if not to set you free from sin and this world, and yet will you hang on to it by calling yourself 'a sinner in recovery' for the rest of your life?"

With that, He showed me what a Hamster Wheel discipline and accountability could become without a goal of deliverance and freedom. Hebrews 12 reveals the course discipline is to take in our lives, where there is a process and a goal, and that goal is not discipline itself. The Writer says, "All discipline for the moment seems not to be joyful, but sorrowful. Yet, to those who have been trained by it, *afterward*, it yields the peaceful fruit of righteousness."

Most growth processes must begin with discipline, and that's a good thing. Discipline 'trains' us, but there must be a goal as with any other training process. Olympic athletes employ discipline as they train, but the goal and the joy is found in taking home the gold medal. From my experiences, I know Solomon would have called continual discipline without reaching the peaceful fruit of righteousness a 'grievous task which God has given the sons of men.'

The reminders of all the verses that spoke of freedom and rest and peace and deliverance kept resurfacing in me. I began to see the sin-management road I was on was a dead-end, go-nowhere street and I started praying for total freedom. I also began preaching this to my similarly afflicted brothers who, like me, were living life on the dreaded Hamster Wheel. Am I saying I'm totally free of the 'lusts of the flesh?' No, but that specific temptation that ravaged my soul every moment of every day is now gone. After witnessing how this process delivered me from over 40 years of sin-management, I became a card-carrying deliverance minister myself. I urge you, if you have any persistent sins you can't seem to escape, it could well be a demonic stronghold in your life. Hook up with a good deliverance minister and talk. You have nothing to lose except years of shame and suffering.

For a good basic understanding of deliverance, may I suggest you get Don Dickerman's first book on the subject, *When the Pigs Move In?* True deliverance is nothing to be afraid of. As Don says, "It's not a power encounter, it's a truth encounter." Instances where demonic involvement was invited called permission points are identified and rescinded, and principalities and demons are called forth and reminded they have no choice but to submit to the lordship of Jesus Christ as He commands them to confess, repair their damage, and then leave.

When it comes to recognizing sin in your life, why not avail yourself of every tool in the box God has given you for healing—those 'everythings pertaining to life and godliness?' If you've been on the Hamster Wheel for perhaps years with no effect, what do you have to lose? Do not be content with staying clear of sin or beating it back. Get free and know the joy and peace Jesus said He came to bring you!

Chapter V

A Love to Embrace, an Admonishment to Consider

"Thy rod and Thy staff, they comfort me."
— Psalm 23

According to the opening verse of John 13, Jesus was on a mission at His Passover which was to show His disciples 'the full extent of His love.' Other than the criminal crucified next to Him, where there was a critical time factor involved, you would have trouble finding one person in the Bible who ever received the full extent of Christ's love without also experiencing His persistent, dismantling admonishments. The Communion table is about understanding both.

In his most famous Psalm, David revealed he knew the comfort of understanding and embracing both God's rod *and* his staff. He moved in and out of life-threatening circumstances few in our society today would ever encounter, and it was the balance of the rod and the staff of

A Love to Embrace, an Admonishment to Consider • 59

God that allowed him to walk through his literal 'valleys of the shadow of death' without fear. If we use our Shepherd's rod [admonishment] and staff [love], we will do likewise when we join Him at His table.

The shepherd's staff was used for three purposes: drawing the sheep into the herd, bringing them in for close-up inspection, and thereafter guiding them as they moved along. What a perfect picture of Communion: the Holy Spirit bringing us together, helping us with a penetrating self-exam via 'piercing as far as the division of soul and spirit, of both joints and marrow, judging the thoughts and intentions of the heart' (Heb. 4), and finally guiding us through life as we move out, washed clean!

The rod had two purposes: it was most often used as a protective weapon to keep predators away but could also be used to punish the sheep who didn't get the gentler message of the staff. Throughout Scripture the rod, or the scepter, symbolizes authority and is used to discipline the unruly. Proverbs says he who spares the rod hates his son. In Hebrews 1, the scepter of Jesus' kingdom symbolizes righteousness and a disdain for lawlessness, and He never shied away from wielding either. This dynamic duo was on full display at His Passover. We could say they represented the love of God we were to embrace and the admonishments of God we dared not ignore. Together, the rod and the staff of God make for a complete meal and draw the fell picture of the likeness of the One who zealously oversees it.

In Colossians 1, Paul outlines what should be the goal of every administrator at the table for his flock, "We proclaim Him, admonishing every man and teaching every man with all wisdom, so that we may present every man complete in Christ. For this purpose, also I labor, striving according to His power which mightily works within me." We are here to present every participant complete in Christ, and that cannot be done by teaching the half-Christ of grace without truth, and love without admonishment. The Holy Spirit will be with us in power if we take up this double-edged sword of God to fight the good fight against the cover-ups, denials, and rationalizations that have rendered the troubling polling numbers we see today amongst churchgoers. Like his Master, there was no timidity or hesitation in Jesus or Paul to wield admonishment and speak truth into the darkness. There should be none in our Communion administrators either.

Jesus disciplines us for our good to keep us humble, repentant and, therefore, teachable. The words He spoke and the deeds He displayed during the Passover, together, were a perfect representation of the '*full extent* of His love.' Without the former, you get legalism. Without the latter, you get—well, you get the polling results that show how akin we have become to the Laodicean church.

The Full Passover Account

In all Gospel accounts, the first act of Jesus at the Passover meal was to identify Judas as His betrayer when He said, "[The betrayer] is he who will dip his bread in the cup with me." In John 13:2, we find these words, signifying that at that point in time the Passover had begun. Likewise, in all gospel accounts, the ceremony concludes with Jesus leading His disciples over the Brook Kidron to the Garden of Gethsemane.

In all other gospels save John's, the Passover accounts are but small paragraphs. However, the crossing of Kidron in John occurs at the beginning of chapter 18. If you compare John's account to the other Gospels, you will find that *all that transpired between John 13 and 18 occurred at the Passover*! Here is by far the most complete account of Jesus' teaching and conduct at this critical event, and it beautifully paints a picture of the balance of love and admonition.

> [Author's Note: There is a controversial verse at the end of John 14, where Jesus says, "Arise, let us be going." It is found nowhere in any of the other gospel accounts. While theories exist concerning this statement there is no indication that circumstances changed, or of any movement from the group between this point and John 18.]

Chapter V

Why is it so important to understand the account of the Passover in John? I believe the most focused, powerful teaching of Jesus' entire ministry unfolded that very night, including:

- His proclamation of being the way, the truth, and the life.
- The prophecy of His death, resurrection, and return to the throne.
- The most focused account in all the gospels foretelling the work and character of the Holy Spirit coming to succeed Him, which impacts all of us who came after more than any single fact.
- The Vine and Branches: His restatement of the Great Commandment and the picture of the balanced life of the disciple.
- Prophecies concerning coming persecutions for the disciples, and,
- Reassurances of the character and love of the Father for them.

In addition to Jesus' teaching, consider the impact of His deeds at the Passover:

- The washing of feet: Jesus' first act was to bow and cleanse the feet of the disciples as He showed them one last time the Master was there 'not to be served, but to serve.' He then told them to follow this example by serving one another. This was part of another message he wanted to leave for all who would come before His table of sacrifice for ages to come.

- In general, the cleansing of the fellowship. His next act was to confront Judas, this 'devil in their midst,' releasing him without delay to accomplish His evil deed. Jesus was about to impart the most important teaching of His ministry on earth, and just as Paul instructed us, we must forewarn or remove those unworthy to partake. This means that the *first two acts of Jesus at the Passover were to ensure the cleansing of the fellowship.* I will spend a great deal of time discussing Judas and how we have ignored our responsibilities to fence the table properly, thus opening ourselves to the justifiable judgment of God. Would that our administrators today note how carefully Jesus guarded His proceedings and do likewise.

- Confronting sin: Jesus made it absolutely clear Communion was to be a time of righteous confrontation. His earthly existence neared an end, and the curtain fell on superficiality of any kind. After dismissing Judas, He turned to Peter as the disciple delivered his 'I'll defend you to the end' speech. Jesus no-doubt glared at him and told him that most certainly Peter would rather deny Him. When Phillip asked Jesus to show them the Father, he likewise became the target of Jesus' rebuke as He questioned Phillip's knowledge of His words and his understanding of who He was.

Jesus had a message to impart to them that all of life would hang upon, and He had a prayer for them that all of life would come from. It was time to chew on every word He spoke and consider every move He made. It was a time for reverent observance of the Man and the ceremony.

- The high priestly prayer: The final act of Jesus among them was to seal His disciples through intercessory prayer. Through this act, He handed over to them the keys to the kingdom of heaven on earth [see my book: *The Kingdom Election*]. In this final display of incomprehensible love and grace, God entrusted His perfect plan into the hands of imperfect people He knew would spend their lives in a titanic struggle pitting flesh against spirit. The charge was passed from the Father, to the Son, and on to the disciples in a prayer that would forever anoint them for their mission on earth.

Throughout John's Passover account, there is a noticeable pattern to Christ's teachings found in His balanced approach to love/forgiveness/grace and discernment/warning/admonition. Jesus always taught this way, which makes sense inasmuch as He was the One who came to save the world and also the One who came to judge it.

We see this balance of truth and grace in the characteristics the early churches displayed (Acts 9). They "enjoyed peace, were built up, and moved forward in the *fear* of the Lord *and* the *comfort* of the Holy Spirit." Solomon tells us, "By mercy and truth iniquity is atoned for, and by the fear of the Lord we are able to keep from evil" (Prov. 16). Job says, "For He inflicts pain and gives relief—He wounds, and His hands also heal" (Job 15), and Paul says, "Behold then the kindness and severity of God" (Rom. 11). Tearing to heal, wounding to bandage, breaking down to revive, and striking to raise up that we may live righteously before Him (Hos. 6) has always been God's way. Through grace *and* truth iniquity is atoned for. Through the fear of the Lord *and* the comfort of the Holy Spirit, the church is kept from evil, increases in numbers, and enjoys peace.

Need we be reminded that our greatest example of God striking to heal is Jesus Himself, who was crushed and pierced for our iniquity? Isaiah tells us that the chastening for our redemption would fall upon Him, and by His injury we would be healed (Isa. 53). Could there be any greater example of the most severe striking [admonishment] in history ever inflicted, and all to bring about the greatest healing [love] ever accomplished than the Lamb who was Slain?

Chapter V

The Two Critical Questions

Two questions should be posed every time we come to The Lord's Table: first, is there love that needs to be embraced and, second, is there an admonishment that needs to be considered?

As to the first question, Jesus says to the church at Ephesus, "I know your deeds and your toil and perseverance, and that you cannot tolerate evil men, and you put to the test those who call themselves apostles, and they are not, and you found them to be false. And you have persevered and have endured for My name's sake. You have not grown weary. But I have this against you: that you have left your first love" (Rev. 2). The church had gotten the admonishment and discipline down, showed great discernment in dealing with the enemy, and displayed the endurance James tells us leads to perfection. But they had evidently forgotten to continue in the love of Jesus they had once known, leading to a religious spirit or hard-heartedness in one form or another.

Referring back to Galatians 1 in addressing the second question, Paul spoke of *admonishing every man and teaching every man* with all wisdom, so that every man might be complete in Christ. So much of scripture is admonishing in nature, but we cannot live by admonishment alone any more than we could live by grace alone. We would lose heart and grow weary in our pursuit of Christ. No, a balance of both is needed—qualities Jesus both taught and modeled at His Passover.

A Love to Embrace, an Admonishment to Consider • 67

When we examine all the verses in the New Testament that deal with the Passover/Communion [approximately 241 in all], we find that approximately 54 of them are neutral commentary, 59 of them espouse God's grace and love, 103 are instructional, and 25 are admonishing in nature, to wit:

- John 13:4-17: Washing of the disciples' feet [love to embrace]
- Verse 10: Judas is singled out as one with a hard heart [an admonishment to consider]
- Verse 18-30: Judas dismissed [an admonishment to consider]
- Verse 31-37: Peter rebuked for boasting [an admonishment to consider]
- John 14:1-7: Jesus comforting the disciples [love to embrace]
- Verse 8-11: Philip's rebuke for his lack of faith [an admonishment to consider]
- Verse 15-31: Jesus promising the Holy Spirit [love to embrace]
- John 15:1-17: The teaching of the vine and branches—the balanced life of the disciple [mixture of love to embrace and admonishments to consider]
- Verse 18-27 and John 16:1-4: The warning of persecutions to come [an admonishment to consider]
- John 16:5-29: Promises of the coming Spirit and His resurrection [love to embrace]
- John 17: The high priestly prayer [love to embrace]

Jesus knew of the existence of His apostle's sinful natures, the temptations facing them in the world, and the hardships and persecutions they would confront from it all. He also knew this balance of admonishment and love together would be necessary to carry them through.

Tough Words Concerning Tough Love

I close this chapter with the Lord speaking through His prophet Malachai to those administrators of His holiest of altars who were not properly fencing it through tough love. These warnings are very applicable to what has caused contemporary Communion services to be the tepid, ineffective ceremonies they are today. He begins, "'You are presenting defiled food upon My altar.' But you say, 'How have we defiled Thee?' in that you say, 'The Table of the Lord is to be despised.' But when you present the blind for sacrifice, is it not evil? And when you present the lame and sick, is it not evil'" (Mal. 1)? 'Blind, lame, and sick' sound familiar? How about 'weak, sick, and asleep?'

Malachi continues, "'But now, will you not entreat God's favor that He may be gracious to you? With such an offering on your part, will He receive any of you kindly?' says the Lord of Hosts. 'Oh, that there were one among you who would shut the gates that you might not uselessly kindle fire on My altar! I am not pleased with you,' says the Lord of Hosts, 'nor will I accept an offering from you!'"

A Love to Embrace, an Admonishment to Consider • 69

God has given us the perfect instrument to clean the table of His new tabernacle—the one that dwells in our hearts and minds, But He asks a piercing question of those who would administer it: "Who among my shepherds will heed My words to Malachai and follow My Son's example? Who will have the courage and conviction of My Word to be watchmen at the gates, and stand against those who would defile My altar by coming with impure, unrepentant hearts?" Can we honestly look at the condition of the church in America and fail to see the severity of the judgments God is currently employing to try to get our attention?

Malachi concludes His message: "But as for you, you have turned aside from the way. You have caused many to stumble by [your] teaching...You are not keeping My ways but are showing partiality in the instruction." When we make the altar all about grace and neglect to include the admonishments that are equally a part of it—when we fail to show the *full extent of Jesus' love* we do indeed 'show partiality in the instruction.' When our administrators do that, they *turn aside* from the biblical path and take their sheep with them.

As we approach The Table of the Lord, let us reverently consider the mood, the attitude, the spirit, and the awesome power of Jesus' Passover meal! Let us realize that no other venue could have been selected to contain it and meditate on the totality of Christ's actions and message. Jesus still confronts us there with an admonishment that we need to consider, and He still forgives us there with a love we need to embrace. There, He still intercedes in High Priestly prayers for us and seeks to bring unity among us 'so that the world may know His Father sent Him.' At the Communion table, Jesus still perfectly prepares and maintains us for the daunting task of trying to live in holiness and enduring faith in a fallen world. Let us not go on tipping the scales but rather embracing the balance!

Chapter VI

Prodigals, Fathers, and Brothers

> If you allow a clown to rule in your palace,
> the clown does not become a king.
> Your palace becomes a circus.
> — Ancient Turkish Proverb

The story the Prodigal Son offers us is a dramatic representation of one of Communion's primary functions: bringing the lost sheep of God's house in from a life of wandering. It reveals the heart of the Father for all His prodigals, along with the attitudes those more mature need to embrace as they do His work.

The story begins with a man who had two sons, the younger who wanted to take his share of the father's estate and go off on his own. Like the older brother, he was nothing less than a full-blown blood relative and heir. But the younger decided to squander his inheritance in favor of a life of rebellion, while the older decided to stay home, living in obedience to the rules of his father's house.

Christian men are sons of their Heavenly Father and heirs of His kingdom, yet they are also sons of Adam and heirs of his fallen-ness. As sons of our Father, we listen to what He has to say to us through His Word and personal revelation. As heirs, we try to extend the legacy of His house. As sons of Adam, though, we can also be apathetic, abandon our responsibilities, become disobedient, and wander off on our own journeys. Being ever the loving and faithful One, our God does as his counterpart in the story and grants us our free will.

Those who have had prodigal sons know that letting go can be the hardest thing in the world to do. You know they are leaving your care terribly ill-equipped to face the world because they feel they have all the answers when they've proven they don't. They exist in a dream world that precludes them from godly, or even rational, thinking and rebel against authority simply because it is authority: spiritual or earthly. Any attempts to keep them at home will only serve to widen the chasm already causing gaping wounds in the relationship. From a spiritual standpoint, people leave God's path because they have somehow become numb to Him and embraced other lovers: the world, idols, their pride, etc. When they reject all attempts to call them back, we must let them go to the school of hard knocks for a season where, hopefully, they will come to their senses.

After his dad's money had been frittered away, the prodigal entered that school and had to go to work feeding pigs. His working conditions and menial pay led him to long to be treated as well as the pigs, yet no one seemed to care. Prodigals squander so many good things as they wander off: relationships with both God and people suffer, any clear view of the kingdom becomes blurred, and they allow the enemy to 'steal, kill, and destroy' their heritage through ongoing sinful lifestyles.

Such foolish pursuits inevitably lead to famine, for without God and spiritual family in their lives the provision, peace, security, guidance, and love they once enjoyed abandons them. If, at that point, they fail to realize their foolishness, and repent and return, substitutes inevitably capture their interests. They attach themselves to just about anything that will satisfy the widening black hole swirling within their souls. As hard as they try to embrace what the world serves up, the satisfaction they knew in a loving family escapes them and they become relegated to feeding with swine instead of dining at the family table.

Fortunately, this son comes to his senses, realizing even the lowest of his father's servants fared far better than he was. He repents, returns, and desires only a place far lower on the pecking order back home than he previously enjoyed. When any of us finally realize the trap the enemy has set for us, and come to our senses, we can return in repentance and humility to our Maker, asking Him only to grant us what we should have been satisfied with all along. In the pride that drove us from Him, we wanted something more than He was willing to give. Loyalty to the patience and self-discipline our journey to the kingdom requires gave way to the desires for instant gratification the world uses to draw us away. We wanted to eat from the forbidden tree and ascend to the heights to be gods over our own lives.

A Step He Won't Take for Us

The Prodigal's father then sees his son while he is still some distance from his gate, knows repentance has born its desired fruit, feels compassion for him, and comes running excitedly to embrace him! After the critical step of repentance, in both word and deed, he could experience his father's love and join the family once more. But the son had to swallow his considerable pride and put feet on his repentance to begin the journey back.

All the intentions of changing—all the words of repentance mean little more than meaningless repetition if we fail to act upon them. Anyone who has worked with addicts knows they will fill the air with their 'sorrys' and false promises to change, typically after their addiction has taken them to the bottom of new, and even deeper, pits. They'll repent with trembling voices spoken through many tears before both God and man. But those who have been burned by them have seen this scenario played out before, perhaps many times, and their words fall on deaf ears apart from visible evidence.

12-Step counselors, therapists, and recovery ministers know that few of these tortured souls really mean it and are truly ready to act upon their remorse. This is why the 'make amends' step is required, for it indicates a real desire to put feet on their words. When we follow words of repentance with the actions that prove our intent to change is genuine, the door always opens to our Father's gate.

But don't miss the fact that, while the father searched the horizon for his son's return, he wasn't about to venture beyond the gate. He wasn't going to chase the son, begging him to return. Our Father puts just such a gate in place to ensure we never mistake Him for the Idol of Grace. He knows there is a fence line around His kingdom He cannot venture beyond if His prodigals are to learn from their mistakes and grow up, and Communion is a great place to discover where that fence line is.

God demands that His children take small steps toward Him in response to the giant step He took toward us. He knows that if He rescued us every time we decided our way was *the* way, we would learn very little and that we would come to rightly believe there were no consequences for wrong choices. But if our repentance is genuine, we won't have to come and be announced at the gate when we return, for our Father will be scanning the horizon every minute of every day, waiting to get out the steaks and fire up the grill! No servant had to notify the prodigal's father that his son approached. They found that out as he knocked them aside while running and shouting, "Slay the calf, grab the sandals, the robe, and the ring! My son...He's back...My son!"

Scanning the Horizon

I remember driving down a street near my home on my way to work back in 1999. As I drove by a park where I had coached little league football and our family had enjoyed picnics, the sounds of sirens suddenly filled the air. I remember hearing a lot of sirens and watching a couple of police cruisers rushing past me as I sat waiting at a stoplight. I drove on to work, thinking little of a few sirens. Upon arriving, however, I heard the horrid news from everyone there as they huddled around the television set, faces creased with masks of disbelief.

The park I was driving by was Clement Park. The city was Littleton, Colorado, and that ominously strange day was April 20. The high school that stood in view on the other side of the park was Columbine, and unbeknownst to me at the very moment I was driving by two tortured sons of Satan were on a murderous rampage that shocked the world. Thirteen died that day in a hail of bullets not two miles from my home, the first of which was a kid I had coached in little league. It was to be 'a day that would live in infamy.'

At that time, Jim, a devoted family man whose kids went to Columbine, and I were involved in a fellowship group together at church. His son had also played with mine on the little league team he helped me coach. Jim's wife was our team mom—you know, both the kind of parents who loved being involved in the lives of their children. They had a son who was one of the first to get out on that fateful morning and a daughter who was not so fortunate. She was trapped in the now infamous science room, watching a popular teacher slowly bleed to death before her eyes and was one of the last ones out.

Jim and his wife first heard about the attack at around 11:30 a.m. All the parents were told to go to a local elementary school and wait for word of the dispositions of their children. I found out a couple of days later that my friends agonized for almost five hours before the very last bus came in with their daughter on it. There were other parents there who would never stop waiting and watching for children who would not come home again. Were Jim and his wife 'standing by the gate, scanning the horizon?' Only a parent can even begin to imagine the sheer terror of those hours when they fear injury or death of their children.

This is such a beautiful metaphor to the story of the prodigal and the Communion celebration, for the story and the ceremony are all about the dead coming to life and the lost being found. When God sees us in a state of life-restoring repentance, the 'calf' of the body and the blood can be prepared on our behalf. But not until 'the knife' of self-examination has been employed and real steps toward repentance taken.

Stealing the Calf?

In John 10 Jesus speaks of Himself being the gate to the sheepfold, and anyone who enters via another way is a 'thief.' I wonder what the father's reaction would have been had the son tried to sneak back, hungry but unrepentant, to steal the calf from its stall? Would there have been a feast prepared then for the prodigal, or judgment? Had he refused his own self-examination that led him to repent and return, what would the father's reaction have been then? By partaking unworthily, would he not have been 'eating judgment upon himself?' Yet this is precisely what we do to God when we come to His table as *thieves of grace*—wanting to steal the forgiveness the Passover offers without doing our part in the partnership to merit it. If an end-around of any kind is attempted at Communion's gate of repentance 'weakness, sickness, and spiritual death' can and will ensue.

Unfortunately, thieves of grace in the church today are more common that repentant sons. I do not blame the sheep for this any more than Jesus did. One of the reasons I write this book is to keep God's just judgment from coming down on those to whom the stroke was then, and is now, truly due: administrators who have improperly taught and overseen the table, allowing the sheep to remain lost in the Father's very house. The Idol of Grace that, in turn, has birthed many thieves of grace at the Communion table. In his timeless book on what disciples should look like, *The Cost of Discipleship*, Dietrich Bonhoeffer says:

> Cheap grace is grace we bestow on ourselves. Cheap grace is the preaching of forgiveness without requiring repentance, baptism without church discipline, **Communion without confession,** *and absolution without personal confession...* **the word of cheap grace has been the ruin of more Christians than any commandment of works.** [emphasis mine]

When it comes to Communion, Bonhoeffer's last statement could not be more spot-on. Grace has become, as he forewarned, a blessing we 'bestow upon ourselves' to call upon whenever we need it to rationalize our sin, and this apart from true repentance. It is an idol because it does *our* bidding rather than the one true God who demands we do *His* bidding. We order our idol to excuse us when God offers no such easy escape route and orders us to, in partnership with Him, take the hard road of shoe-leather repentance.

The Idol of Grace finds his genesis in a false definition of the word [Greek: charis] that has been preached over decades, that being 'unmerited favor.' Under this definition, we can live any way we want, soil the name of Christ with our words and deeds, and be more worldly than godly, and all is forgiven. It is, after all, 'unmerited,' right? Once we 'pray the prayer' grace has us and won't ever let go because it's about our loving, doting Savior and not us. This is Philippians 2:8-9 devoid of verse 10. It's 'confessing Christ with our mouths' without 'believing on Him with our hearts' (Rom. 10). It is proclaiming our 'Lord, Lords' without doing what He says (John 6), and what James calls dead faith devoid of evidence (Jas. 2).

The Idol of Grace with 'unmerited favor' in hand has birthed the 'clown' that has been allowed to enter, and now rule, the palace of our modern Communion services. True to the Turkish proverb, when it assumed its throne, the palace built upon 'deed and truth' became the circus built upon 'word and tongue.' This has created millions of court jesters in the place of loyal citizens ever since.

The true definition of charis is the divine touch upon the heart of a person *AND* the evidence of that touch in his life thereafter. "The Word of God: living, active, sharp, piercing to the very depths of our souls, and able to judge the thoughts and intentions of the heart" (Heb. 4) profoundly impacts us. When we invite the Holy Spirit into our lives, He reaches into every crevice of life and completely changes us, which then must result in a radical, manifest departure from who we were in the past.

This transformation requires our amen with more than mere words. It *demands* the evidence of the divine touch He alone can provide because, as Paul proclaimed, "It is no longer we who live but Christ who lives in us, and the *lives* we now *live*, we *live* by faith in the Son of God" (Gal. 2). You cannot have Christ living in you through the Spirit and not *live* life as though He is present. Deeds in the body of a man will follow naturally what is going on in his soul. But under the false definition and the lordship of the Idol of Grace, those deeds are not required as evidence of grace.

Over years of religious teachings we have belittled holiness and truth, and magnified grace, to where neither holds its original meaning or power and neither is able to save. We think we can remain unrepentant as we daily indulge our 'Little Preciouses' that feed our flesh, and yet walk with Jesus and be forgiven. ***Repentance 'in deed and in truth' has become token and insincere homage in our evangelism, request without demand in our preaching, and a lost utensil in the place-setting of our holy Communions.*** Without a sincere and humble response to God's conviction in our heart-of-hearts, grace upon the lips or in the mind becomes the problem and not the solution.

In 1 Samuel 24, David is told by God to go to a place to offer up a sacrifice in order that a prophesied plague might be averted. When David tells the owner of the place, a God-fearing man, the reason for his coming, the man tells him to use whatever he wants at no charge. David replies, "No, but I will surely buy it from you for a price, for I will not offer burnt offerings to the Lord my God which cost me nothing." Oh, that we would stop presenting offerings to the Lord our God as prodigals at His holy table that cost us nothing! Grace was free when we first experienced it, but it is not costless as we now grow in it.

When we come to the table carrying unconfessed sin that we refuse to deal with, through both confession and action, we become thieves of the grace that was prepared before us in the body of Christ at Calvary, and role-players in the clown's circus. Let us reject this idol and return our palace to its original intent of being a house of holiness.

What of the Older Son?

The story of the prodigal now turns to another type of person regularly attending Communion services: the older son who had stayed home faithfully serving his father. *In Remembrance of Truth and Grace* is about bringing back sheep lost in our Father's house, and that includes both sons in our story. The older brother became understandably upset when told a great feast was in the works because his useless younger brother had returned. He decided to throw what amounted to a temper tantrum, refusing to go back to the house to join in the festivities. Upon hearing this, his father left the party and went out to find him.

When the two got together, the older son made a case for his years of fealty and asked why his father had never thrown such a celebration on his behalf? He then proceeded to list the litany of offenses of which his younger brother had been guilty. Given the history between them, he wondered why his father was so excited about the younger son's return, to which the father replied, "My child, you have always been with me, and all that is mine is yours. We had to be merry and rejoice, for this brother of yours was dead and has begun to live. He was lost and has been found!"

Ah, the older son: so often vilified for being such a poor sport. The prodigal story is about more than just the less mature struggling to renew a relationship with God. It's as much about those more mature understanding their role in the body and the Communion process. Rather than joining the father in welcoming the younger son back, the older brother forgot the disciple's calling and, yes, acted more like a prodigal himself. He displayed pride and jealousy, and even viewed His good works done for his father as 'slaving.' In this he was wrong, but at least the older son enjoyed an enduring relationship with his father that had provided a foundation between them the prodigal, returned or not, did not enjoy. And for that, the father treated the two sons very differently.

Most notably, in his dealings with the younger son the father refused to chase and patiently waited for conviction to run its course. But when the older son began to stray, the father immediately *left the celebration for the prodigal* and pursued him. So, who was the priority here? No line existed between the two because the older son had not caused the need for one, so the father chased him down to explain what was going on.

In one of His Passover teachings, Jesus said, "You are My friends *if* you do what I command you. No longer do I call you slaves, for the slave does not know what his master is doing. But I have called you friends, for all things that I have heard from My Father I have made known to you" (John 15). The younger son was a 'slave' in this story, and the older son had proved himself a 'friend.' Therefore, the father 'pleaded with him,' explaining what he was doing as promised. He reassured the older son that the two were joined at the hip and everything the father owned was also his because he had always proved himself a faithful son and servant. And notice, there was no prodigal's repentance required. The elder son never said he was sorry or acknowledged he had sinned against his father, for his lifetime of evidence made the words unnecessary. This one was a trusted co-worker who just needed to be reminded of that fact.

If you are one of Jesus' 'older sons,' who, though you stumble at times remain a saint in training striving daily to walk the path of discipleship, understand that for the most part Communion's warnings aren't for you. Paul said the law was good for the lawful and was not employed for the righteous man, but rather for the lawless and rebellious (1 Tim. 1). Though the need for repentance never abandons us—and even mature disciples need to employ the table to pause and take stock—as older sons, they are always welcome to the Father's feast to enjoy the body of Christ and minister to the less mature in attendance.

'The laws' of Communion are about restoring all those less mature who don't know what Jesus is doing, have lost their spiritual compass, and need to find it again. It is forever our mandate to 'bear one another's burdens,' seeing to it that all of God's sons and daughters shed their clown costumes, put on their crowns, and receive true grace and healing in the palace of Christ's ultimate sacrifice.

Chapter VII

The Soma: The Body of Christ

"So also you, since you are zealous of spiritual gifts, seek to abound for the edification of the church."
— (1 Cor. 14)

For God, nothing takes the priority over His bride—not when Jesus came to earth and not now. He will admonish, teach, correct, and train her relentlessly until that glorious day when she stands fully united with Him for eternity. Perhaps this is why His most sacred and powerful ceremony was provided exclusively for His body. Given the importance of the Ecclesia, it's not surprising there are very few topics the New Testament spends more time on than our place in, our conduct toward, and our involvement within it. In my book, *The Kingdom Election* [available in eBook, print, and audio], I devote an entire chapter to what I call the ultimate expression of the kingdom of heaven on earth, which is His people living in unity and truth in authentic community.

I believe Paul weaved into his Communion instruction the way for the church to realize and maintain these lofty goals, for at His table God convicts those who have become lost in His house to wake up and return to fellowship. Then, they can begin to contribute their unique gifts for its edification rather than living for themselves on the sidelines as spectators to their highest calling in life.

Ministering to All in the Body

Through many years of ministry, I have observed five basic types of people who claim to follow Christ. These types generally follow the pattern of the seeds of the Sower, along with one additional category. Ministering to all of them likewise takes all types in the body. They are:

- The babes [first seed]: These are the recent converts who are excited about their newfound faith, and many times are much more open and bolder about sharing it with others than the next two groups. However, they need to be mentored by those more mature because they are extremely vulnerable to the deceptions and temptations of the evil one at this stage in their walks. Their roots haven't had time to develop because they simply need sufficient time to come to understand and move into an abiding relationship with Christ and His Holy Spirit. Doing so in the kilns of experience will provide their identity, their purpose, and entrance into the of heaven Jesus joined to earth.

For these, Communion presents a wonderful opportunity to observe and participate in the setting most conducive to witnessing how mature believers are to conduct themselves within the body. They can join in this most real of all Christian events that will take them beyond the 'elementary principles of repentance from former works and faith in God' (Heb. 5-6), and on to the meatier fare of understanding and discernment. Being able to discern their own shortcomings early on in their walk will be a tool that will serve them well from then on.

- The perpetual babes [second seed]: The next two groups comprise and characterize the lost sheep of God's house the writer of Hebrews spoke of who just can't seem to bring themselves to a deeper and more mature faith than the one the Idol of Grace provides. They have missed out on, or become numb to, how to *practice* their faith. Most are churchgoers, but never have become friends with Jesus by seeking a deeper relationship that begins with acting upon His commands.

They display the façade of the believer, but little fruit of the Spirit is visibly present in their lives apart from Sunday mornings. It is all milk and no meat, the fault laying at the feet of a religious system that offers little more than milk on its menu, and them for not taking more responsibility for their own growth. Jesus would ask these people the question, "Why do you call Me 'Lord, Lord,' and yet do not do what I say" (Luke 6)?

Communion for these can be the key that opens the door, because biblical participation in this ceremony *demands* action. It requires serious reflection upon their personal place with God and man and will disclose to them their hypocrisy. This group will find marvelous opportunities to understand the importance of practicing their beliefs as they see others acting on their issues. If they will just accept their Communion responsibilities, the beginnings of the journey from babe to meat-eaters will find purchase in their souls.

- The Laodiceans [third seed]: These are the ones who 'think they are rich and in need of nothing' when nothing could be further from the truth. They think claiming Jesus' name and achieving worldly success somehow pleases Him when little else in their lives lines up. They are neither hot nor cold when it comes to the things that matter to God because worldly security and wealth are their true priorities. To these, Jesus is little more than another trinket to add to their well-stocked shelves of the possessions that are the very weeds choking their faith. Any sin in their lives is quickly rationalized and then dissolved through imbibing in the worldly comfort and security their trappings provide for them.

These first three groups have no problem with modern Communion ceremonies that allow them to cover up practiced sin patterns rather than confronting them. But contrary to what the shepherds of the Idol of Grace teach them, they 'eat and drink the judgment of continued weakness, sickness, and sleep upon themselves' (1 Cor.11) most every time they partake. If not helped to understand the meaning and power of the table, they will remain superficial people, both to the world and the church.

It need not be so, for these folks can find Communion to be the Laodicean buster! Here, they can be taught the dangers of hypocrisy and lukewarmth. Here, they can be gently forced to come face-to-face with a holy God and the confrontational, healing qualities of loving fellowship. Here, the safe and secure world of the Idol of Grace cannot comfort them. They will have to face their shortcomings or admit they are unwilling to, knowing there is such a thing as unworthy participation and consequences. They simply cannot leave from a biblical Communion ceremony in the same delusional state in which they arrived, and that's a good thing.

- Fruit-bearers [fourth seed]: These are those who have learned *and* practiced the balanced life of John 15. They are fully assured He 'knows them' and they know Him. They have elected citizenship in the kingdom of heaven on earth and have formed an abiding relationship with Jesus. They hear the revelatory voice of the Holy Spirit which propels them to relentlessly go out to bear fruit in the body and in the world.

As true saints of a living God, they have learned it is only in fully engaging with the community internally and reaching others externally, letting the love of Jesus that abides in them flow into those lives they touch that makes life worth living. They leave an indelible mark on those they come to know—the mark of the Gospel of their living God. They have forsaken the world and its temptations and think nothing of self, pouring out their lives regularly and consistently for the evangelism of the lost, the discipleship of the saved, and the edification of the body. They are 'friends' who look to the heavens, as Jesus did, and do what their Master does.

Communion for mature followers of Christ is a blessed time of reflection, fine-tuning, and intimate fellowship with both God and man. It is also a wonderful opportunity to do what they always do—what they know they were born to do—fulfill the mission to which the Holy Spirit has called them in being a conduit between God's abundance and the needs of others. There is no better time than Communion for them to come to understand, speak

into, and bear the burdens of their weaker brothers thus fulfilling Jesus' law (Gal. 6) and their ministry.
- The apostates: These are the Judases: those Paul called 'hidden reefs in our love feasts' (Jude 12), those doubly dead and lawless who either never knew God or have become so trapped in sinful practices, pride, and self-deception that they now go out deceiving others with their false dreams, doctrines, and disobedient lifestyles. And make no mistake, Satan seeks to insert them in every fellowship that has cracks in its armor. They appear as 'children of light' but are the clowns in the palace who, if allowed to sully this most holy of ceremonies, will turn it into a deadly circus. Matthew 18 discipline must be employed here for the sake of the body, for there is no place for the apostates in Holy Communion. They must be, as Judas was, 'dismissed with haste' from the proceedings. Jesus found it necessary and so should we.

It is absolutely critical administrators of this most holy ceremony be able to identify these different people within their flocks, and teach and act accordingly, which is one reason why Communion should be observed in small groups where maturity levels have already manifested themselves. Push too hard on those not ready, or back off too soon on those who need the push, and valuable fruit can be wasted.

The Book of Fellowship

It is no mere coincidence that Paul's Communion instructions are found ensconced in the context of 1st Corinthians, because it is *the* epistle dealing with the body of Christ, to wit:

- Chapters one and three contain instructions and warnings concerning divisions in the body.
- Chapter five concerns how to administer church discipline and the mandate we have to be righteously judgmental within the body.
- Chapter six includes Paul's lament over lawsuits in the body.
- Chapters eight and ten discuss our liberties in, and causing stumbling amongst, the members of the body.
- Chapters ten and eleven speak to the maintenance of the members of the body, and thus the body itself, through proper participation in Holy Communion.
- Chapter eleven discusses the place of man and woman in the body.
- Chapters twelve through fourteen provide extensive teaching on the use and abuse of spiritual gifts in the body, along with Paul's structure for the apostolic church.
- Chapter sixteen speaks of the financial support of the body.

It follows, then, that Communion would deal not only with the individual's place with Christ, but also his place within the body. The word *body* [Greek: soma] carries two meanings, both of which are included here. Without fully grasping both, we can believe we are guilty of sinning only against Christ's sacrifice on the Cross—*His* body alone—by unworthily partaking of the elements. To believe this is to understand only part of the truth. *Soma* also means the body as a whole: a closely united group that comes to form a unified culture. There is strong evidence in his Communion instruction that Paul wasn't talking exclusively about how we share in Christ's literal body, he was also speaking of the importance of how we share in the ecclesia!

Breaking it down: in 1st Corinthians 10 Paul gives us a preamble to the Communion teaching immediately to follow when he asks, "Is not the cup of blessing with which we bless a sharing in the blood of Christ? Is not the bread which we break a sharing in the body of Christ? Since there is one bread, we who are many are one body, for we all partake of the one bread." We could say the first *soma* referred to is the body of Christ Himself because it is tied directly to His blood. However, proceeding on to the second reference, we see that Paul compares Christ's body—standing alone now as the bread—to His body-corporate through our breaking of it together.

It is through Christ's broken body [*His* soma] that we can now all be one restored body [the *corporate* soma] in the sharing of that sacrifice. By employing both meanings,

The Soma: The Body of Christ • 95

Paul makes the body of Christ-personal that we participate in the same as the body of Christ-corporate we are likewise to participate in. The two cannot be separated. The broken physical body becomes the food of the restored church body that was born of the sacrifice we are to remember at the Communion table.

Paul refers to the two meanings again in the Communion instruction itself (1 Cor. 11). In verses 27 and 28, Paul uses the body and blood of the Lord together, thus signifying Christ's personal sacrifice. However, in verse 29, Paul's message once again changes. Notice here that the blood is missing, and the body is mentioned alone. Like he did in chapter 10, he starts with the body and blood, and then leaves the blood out, thereby transforming the meaning of *soma* from personal to corporate. I believe Paul is saying, as a part of our self-exam, we need to look at how our lives proclaim Christ's sacrifice and, just as importantly, how we contribute to the body-corporate!

Paul also speaks to what happens when we ignore our responsibility to the body by remaining detached or weak, sick, and asleep, as some were then and many are today: "When one member of the body suffers, all members suffer with it" (1 Cor 12). On the other hand, what could it look like when all are healthy as many more could be if we were taking advantage of biblical Communion to renew us to that responsibility? "If one member is honored, all the members rejoice with it." The cumulative message of Paul to the Corinthians indicates the proper function coming from our lives honoring both *somas*. This makes sense inasmuch as if we are honoring Christ with our lives individually, we will also be honoring that which was most important to Him: bringing together the lost sheep in His Father's house.

In summary, Paul says in Ephesians 4, "We are to grow up in all aspects into Him who is the head, even Christ, from whom the whole body being fitted and held together by that which every joint supplies according to the proper working of each individual part, causing the growth of the body for the building up of itself in love." The individual is strengthened to fit into the body, thereby strengthening it. But weak, sick, and asleep members make for a dysfunctional body. John Eldredge has this to say in his book *Wild at Heart*:

> There is no other man who can replace you in your life, in the arena you've been called to. If you leave your place in line, it will remain empty. No one else can be who you are meant to be.

God knew that any fellowship, no matter the size, would function only as well as the sum of its parts did. Remove the $10.00 oil filter from a $350,000 Ferrari, and even if every other part is functioning perfectly a magnificent supercar will become a glorified paperweight in very short order. There are no unimportant members in the fellowship of the saints—no members we can afford to leave in a perpetual state of immaturity and 'no man to be left behind' if the soma is going to fulfill her mandate on this earth!

Sins of Omission and Commission

My focus up to now has been upon sins of *commission*, that is, the sin we commit through what we do via our sinful thoughts, words, or deeds. Yet when it comes to the soma, where most fall is through acts of *omission*, or what we fail to do: gifts we fail to discover, develop, and deploy.

When considering our Communion self-examination, we need to consider acts we are omitting as well as those we are committing, for merely cleaning out our own closet does not necessarily mean proactively moving forward in making a positive contribution to the soma. James spoke of a *positive* way to deal with sin—the other side of the repentance coin and it has everything to do with the body-corporate. He says, "My brethren, if any among you strays from the truth and one turns him back, let him know that he who turns a sinner from the error of his way will save his soul from death, and will cover a multitude of sins" (Jas. 5). Here is the body working together for healing and the forgiving of sins through biblical *proactivity*. Communion was tailor-made to bear the fruit of personal repentance through one member of the body turning another from his error. It employs both sides of the perfect coin in assuring the forgiveness of sins.

In summary, I believe Paul is telling us that when we fail to observe the total spirit of Communion correctly, we transgress against Christ's personal sacrifice *and* the body-corporate as well. Given the lack of much resembling authentic Christian community today, it is something we desperately need to reawaken at the Communion table!

A Return to the Exodus

One of the most fascinating comparisons between the Passover of the Exodus and our Communion ceremonies today concerns this issue of our function within the body and how that affects her well-being. When the Death Angel went through Egypt anyone, Egyptian or Israelite, caught outside the Passover ceremony would die. If he were not found within his proper place in the community under the cross of the Passover Lamb's blood on the doorposts, an eternal price would be paid.

But what brought the Death Angel to Egypt in the first place? What was the sin so grievous in God's eyes that He was willing to take such extreme measures to get the attention of not only the Egyptians, but of His people as well? God told Moses to tell Pharaoh that reason was because he refused to let Israel's first-born sons leave to go on a sacred journey, and so in return He would take all of Egypt's first-born sons (Exod. 4). The grievous sin of Pharaoh and his people was their refusal to release the Israelites to worship Him through embarking on a journey of obedience that would take them out of slavery and on to The Promised Land.

Furthermore, what was Pharaoh's attitude that made him so stubbornly resist the pleas of Moses for the release of God's people? According to Exodus 6, 'Pharaoh's heart had become hardened' and so he did not listen to the Lord. Pharaoh was a proud king who ignored the persistent, apparent, and overwhelming call of God—stubbornly refusing to give in to His divine will.

How does this scenario compare to believers today who neglect the overwhelming biblical mandate to be in a constant process of maturity, stop dabbling in sin and loving worldliness, to gather in community, deal with transgression, love proactively, and contribute their gifts to the body? When we compare the circumstances that led to the destruction of the firstborns of Egypt and the weakness, sickness, and 'death' Paul witnessed in Corinth among the faithful, we find sinful practices leading to hard hearts that prohibit the release of God's people to go and worship Him through a journey of obedience that He has predestined for them—a journey that would lead them to the promised land of heaven on earth if they would but go!

The message? "Examine yourself. See what you are doing to My soma, My church, My bride. Judge whether you help or harm her—whether you assist the body in its journey or hold it back. If your contribution is lacking because you are too busy attending to your own selfish needs, or have not cared to develop the gifts I have given you so as to edify it, wake up and repent! Don't harden your heart as Pharaoh did by refusing to deal with your sin and accepting your responsibility to My beloved ecclesia. Beware, for weakness, sickness, and sleep are, like the Death Angel, at your door!"

If the answer to this question proves troubling, fully engaging in the ceremony that bonds the body like no other is precisely where to get back on track. God designed His table to be *the* forum for His children to pursue unity and purpose through loving fellowship. Oh, the perfection of this! ***Communion is about more than just discovering where the individual discerns his or her standing with God. It provides a holistic environment where the individual discovers where he or she is within the collective of the church as well.***

Chapter VIII

The Matthew 5 Alternative

> "Our goals can only be reached through a vehicle of a plan in which we must fervently believe, and upon which we must vigorously act."
> — Pablo Picasso

I have to believe that many would like to get real with God in their lives but just don't understand how or where to start. If they understood that abstinence included 'the vehicle of a plan' they could believe in to bring them victory, then they would be more apt to 'vigorously act' upon that plan. A passage in Matthew 5 I call The Matthew 5 Alternative offers us just such a plan.

Julie [fictitious name] attended her first Communion with us after attending our fellowship for a few months. We were introduced to her by one of the guys in the group who was casually dating her. However, he had no more success at warming up to her than many others who had tried. And many others had tried, for Julie was a very attractive, intelligent young woman. However, those young men described Julie as one who seemed friendly and fun on the surface but had an impenetrable shell blocking access to anything remotely underneath.

We went up to Genesee Mountain above Denver one warm summer night to enjoy Communion around a campfire, and it was Julie's first experience of our reset table. The more I taught concerning the importance of opening to the conviction of the Spirit and abstinence in the presence of cover-ups, the more anxious she became. She flitted from small group to small group during confession/prayer time [discussed fully in later chapters] without saying much to anyone. Finally, as we prepared to partake of the elements and I gave the final admonition to abstain if denials were not dealt with, she stood up and started pacing frantically back and forth. When we passed the elements and completed the service, she honored the ceremony and abstained.

A few minutes later, as we prepared to break camp and head back to town, she came up to me and said, "I have something I need to get off my chest and, after being a part of this, I know I will never be able to take Communion again until I do." This fifteen-year-old then confessed that she had been sexually molested by her babysitter when she was three years old. For twelve years she had never told anyone, save her mother at the time. Not experiencing the pervasive nature of sexual abuse as we do today, mom dismissed it as a childhood fantasy. For all those years, Julie had lived with the shame, the guilt, the anger, and the isolation the enemy had used that moment to mold her life. Now, it all came pouring out in one beautiful, glorious, tear-filled confession!

Hallelujah! Holy pressure! The Communion 'knife' had penetrated the 'bone' that had built up around her soul and the 'marrow' that had been so infected by it, and had hit its mark! The reason behind all the guilt of thinking it was her fault and all the fear of men lodged deep within her soul—fear that had kept her living in a prison, aloof and distant, was now exposed to God's glorious light. The evil one's plans to destroy her life were uncovered and dismantled, and he had to vacate the premises!

Julie had been a faithful churchgoer for some time and had participated in many Communion ceremonies. But the powerless, feel-good rituals had done nothing to heal her, leaving her a slave to her tortured memories. However, through remembrance of truth and grace, Julie knew she could find the strength to tell her secret story, leave the past behind, and walk into new hope with Christ. The subject of this chapter is something else we had discussed that night and how she understood more than just the requirement to come clean. She also knew there was a plan and a way out of her prison. This story bears witness to a vital element of the Communion experience that invites full conviction and yet, at the same time, provides a path to dealing with the consequences in hope. *Matthew 5 provides a way for those with unfinished business to leave the table without guilt now because they have a practical roadmap in hand for victory in the future!*

Remembering 'There'

It is vital that we understand there is an alternative to either unworthy participation or abstinence without a plan that gives us a future. Abstinence, apart from purpose or goal, leads to defeat and that's not what the table is to be about any more than unworthily participating. Both are dead-end streets. Abstinence with a specific purpose, however, provides a solution to the dilemma that comes upon us when our self-exam proves troubling, and our business with God remains unresolved.

Matthew says, "If therefore you are presenting your offering at the altar, and *there remember* that your brother has something against you, leave your offering before the altar and go your way. First, be reconciled to your brother, and then come and present your offering." What does he mean, to 'there remember?' Why would the type of person Matthew is referring to remember someone had something against him at that specific moment? It is obvious that at some point in the past, he had said or done something to offend his brother. It is also obvious that he had somehow rationalized and covered up his transgression so as to forget about it prior to this specific moment.

God knows this sort of thing happens all the time with His sons and daughters who occasionally err. Therefore, He provided a specific time and place to deal with it. Once one understands the purpose and mission of Communion, the answer to 'Why there?' becomes clear. **He has us here** *remember because here, through the self-exam Paul prescribes, is the specific occasion He provided where His Spirit would bring us to remembrance of our transgressions!*

This is no coincidence. If we will but honor the reason for the table, submitting to its admonishments and partaking of its graces, He will bless it by bringing to mind the very things He wants us to confront. If we will go to this incredible, life-transforming altar with the proper perspective on why we are here, He *will* honor it with a response because we will have demonstrated, through obedience, our souls are prepared to receive His promptings.

He will uncover the roadblocks we have allowed to remain hidden in our lives—the barriers that keep us from enjoying the fullest benefits available to us through our relationship with the Spirit of His Son. If we will but let Him, He will 'here' at the table, like nowhere else, reveal these impediments to us.

A Bigger Question

As important as it is to set things right with our brother, I believe there is the larger issue that involves taking time to earnestly seek God's conviction concerning the relationship between Him and us. Paul says, "I do not even examine myself, for I am conscious of nothing against myself, yet I am not by this acquitted. But the one who examines me is the Lord. Therefore, do not go on passing judgment before the time but wait until the Lord comes, who will both bring to light the things hidden in the darkness and disclose the motives of men's hearts" (1 Cor. 4).

Paul tells us precisely why any self-examination must begin with allowing the Great Physician His diagnosis, and that is because we are not capable of being objective judges of our own condition. Notice Paul says that just because he thinks he is clean, that does not acquit him in God's court. Why? God is the only one who can bring to light hidden things and disclose the motivations of our hearts that are behind them.

Peter relays much the same message when he says, "Therefore, I will always be ready to remind you of these things, even though you already know them, and have been established in the truth which is present with you. I consider it right, as long as I am in this earthly dwelling, to stir you up by way of reminder" (2 Peter 1). Like Paul, Peter says even though we know the truth and have been firmly established in it, thereby acknowledging these are believers he's talking to, still he cites the need for all of us to regularly be reminded of those truths. He, like Paul, realized even the most committed of followers were not immune to the temptations of the flesh and the deceptions of our cunning and ever-present enemy that open the door to self-deception.

Once our meaningful *God*-exam is done, the road is paved for a meaningful *self*-exam. Conviction must always begin with the Lord, for until we get that right, any further self-examination can be filled with deceptions. Yes, I tell you:

Jesus, the Judge of men, also needs to be asked the question, "Do You have something against me?" when considering what He may want us to 'here, at His altar, remember.'

The Healing Goal of Abstinence

If we discern there is the work of repentance required, then the second half of The Matthew 5 Alternative is what gives us a plan and hope for a brighter tomorrow. It says, "Leave your offering there before the altar and go your way. First, be reconciled to your brother, and then come and present your offering. Agree with your adversary *quickly*..." Proverbs 6 holds a similar message: "Do this then my son and deliver yourself. Since you have come into the hand of your neighbor, go and humble yourself...Do not give sleep to your eyes, nor slumber to your eyelids, but deliver yourself like a gazelle from the hunter's hand."

At His table, the Holy Spirit reminds us of roadblocks we have erected and then urges us to 'go with haste' and purpose to take care of business before we return to the altar the next time. He knows that a little bit of leaven affects the whole lump, and that we must be free of unconfessed sin to be the 'freedmen' He intended. Oswald Chambers, when teaching on these very verses, says:

> [Jesus] is saying, in essence, "Don't say another word to Me. First be obedient by making things right" ... When Jesus drives something home to you through

> His Word, don't try to evade it. If you do, you will become a religious impostor...Even at the risk of being thought of as fanatical, you must obey what God tells you.

In 12-Step programs, they call this making amends, and that means action is required concerning sin before anyone is going to tell you you're OK.

Even when the warnings of 1st Corinthians are reviewed, without the Matthew 5 alternative being proposed the suffering brother or sister could leave feeling they are unworthy altogether to participate—now and perhaps ever again. Without this option, people can continue on in a self-deceived state when Communion was ordained to nuke self-deceptions! Through explaining the simple plan of leaving your offering [abstaining from the elements now], going and taking care of business, and then returning to the altar the next time with a worthy offering of a cleaned-up life to present participants are given a way to, without shame, reveal and shatter the cover-ups and repair a lot of collateral damage!

The current condition of so many churchgoers living in a weakened condition could change drastically through, simply, a proper understanding of abstinence with the goal of repairing the breaches, resulting in victorious return in our Communion observances. Think about it: when you fail a test and later go back, retake it, and pass, don't you forget all about the failure? In fact, you come to appreciate even more how failure can lead to victory! It's often been said we learn few lessons on mountaintops and many in the valleys of failure and defeat. Once you have successfully navigated The Matthew 5 Alternative, you begin to focus upon the newfound horizons that have opened to you as a result of learning from your failures and having become a better person for it.

Why Not Let the Cup Pass?

Again, Berkhof states:

> Even true believers may not partake of the Lord's Supper under all conditions and in every frame of mind...When a person is conscious of being estranged from the Lord or from his brethren, he has no proper place at a table which speaks of Communion.

To partake or abstain is the only litmus test Communion affords. To partake now because our self-exam has proven us ready [if not perfect] or leave our offering at His altar today to return later in victory, are the *only* righteous choices we have. In either case, there is no sin. To come before the altar without thoughtfully considering the decision to partake or abstain, however, is a sin. Exams are all about helping us discern what we have learned or failed to learn, but we must take them to know which.

Many in the modern church perceive it unthinkable, or some kind of affront to grace, to let the cup pass. ***NO! The only sin and unacceptable way—the only affront to grace at The Lord's Table is to partake blindly when we are unfit!*** The focus should be self-examination in the interest of getting real with God and our brothers and sisters to end cover-ups, rather than participating in the elements to help us be okay with our sin or to keep up appearances.

Believers caught up in sinful behaviors would see a new power to heal, and more, if we returned to the precepts of biblical Communion. We need to 'fervently believe' the challenges we hear there are from the Holy Spirit, per the first part of Matthew 5, and then 'vigorously act' upon them per the second part. I admire those who abstain now and then, as I have had to do myself, with a goal toward purity because I know they have taken the spirit of the reset table seriously. They have gained a clearer understanding of the spirit of Communion, their God, and themselves.

I trust fully in the grace I have seen Jesus grant me in this life. However, understanding I have refused the promptings of the Spirit in some aspect of life, I know partaking would only lead to guilt and, if not acted upon, result in God's judgment, a superficial faith, and a hypocritical lifestyle. I would have refused to be trained by His discipline and would know that I would lack the peaceful fruit of righteousness that comes from it until repentance from the sin and deeds of repentance toward renewal were employed. I believe Paul would call this process 'working out our salvation in fear and trembling' (Phil. 2).

Those who have learned the power of abstinence make tremendous progress toward becoming real with both God and man. Rather than insulting grace, they have shown a profound appreciation of being bought with the price of that grace. They have understood and been faithful to Him through honoring the purpose of His table. Such people will never again entertain the fallout that results from prolonged periods immersed in cover-ups.

God has a different message for each of us, depending upon where we are in our walk with Him. What is important is whether we hear what He is saying and act upon it rather than whether we partake of the elements or not. *If done for the right reasons and in the proper spirit, abstinence and participation are one and the same.* Both are acts of obedience, and both are an indication of a functional partnership with the Spirit in our lives. Reverent abstinence should never be looked upon as failure to participate. No, for those who employ it with a goal of victory at their next observance, abstinence can represent the most fully engaged participants of all!

Abstinence No Crutch

Lastly, abstinence should never be used as a crutch rather than a call to action, and it should only be employed until the next observance. Allowing one to abstain over the same circumstance for an extended period of time is not the intent of Matthew 5. Don't let this become a crutch that allows people to think they are reverently observing the fencing of the table when they are still just running from their problems via a different vehicle. That would result in the worst sort of delusion. Abstinence needs to be employed for a specific purpose, that purpose is to be pursued and accomplished, and then life moves on.

Both Matthew 5 and Proverbs 6 include an element of urgency—of quick resolution. It would be rare that reconciliation of any issue should last longer than until the time you observe the next Communion. Come alongside your brother or sister who has seen fit to abstain, help them see to reconciling 'with haste' whatever it was that caused them to abstain, and be a part of their next ceremony being a victorious one!

Again, the repetitive nature of Communion makes it an ideal setting for consistent, ongoing maintenance of the believer's emotional and spiritual state. If you sense the conviction that something needs to be done or a change needs to be made that you have been resisting, then abstain, take real steps to bring yourself back into God's will, and then return the next time to partake. This is the victory! This is good! This is the way The Matthew 5 Alternative was designed to work!

Causing Stumbling

Before we leave this issue of abstinence, we need to look at its potential effects on the soma as well as the individual. What is a person to do when Communion admonishments are absent because the teaching ends at "Do this in remembrance of Me?" Is he or she to partake, even if found to be personally worthy? While many may think me legalistic for this, I believe there to be an issue rather of love that would lead me to say that such a one, even if personally prepared, should consider abstaining from any Communion where the warnings are ignored. It is for this reason I refrain from partaking during most modern church ceremonies.

Paul's exhortations concerning individual believers regarding others as more important than themselves (Phil. 2) are taken seriously by those truly led by God's love. They understand his heartfelt anxieties over the struggles of others, as he asks, "Who is led into sin without my intense concern" (2 Cor. 11)? Likewise, we observe his passionate joy in the maturing faith of his children in 1st Thessalonians 2 and 3: "For you [our disciples] are our glory and joy...now we really live if you stand firm in the Lord!" Under love's definition in 1st Corinthians 13, one becomes ultimately concerned for giving all away and keeping nothing for self.

Out of this same love of Christ that directed his steps, Paul spoke of how *our* conduct was to be directed to an extent by concern over our weaker brothers (1 Cor. 13). He said that we were to refuse to partake in something that caused the confused and less mature to stumble, even if it was acceptable behavior for us. Was Paul being legalistic here? No, he was being loving. Paul realized that different levels of maturity would always be an issue in the body. He didn't want the mature, who had reached a deeper understanding, to do anything in a weak moment that would cause those less mature to stumble. Enabling others to continue on in disobedience, superficiality, and sinful practices because they witness us go forward and thoughtlessly partake is to do exactly that.

When I find myself at a Communion service where I can't possibly know the hearts of everyone in attendance, what am I doing by partaking when no challenges to employ the knife at all are voiced so as to even be considered by the participants? What if there is a man or woman next to me who is denying the Holy Spirit's convictions because of a heart hardened through perhaps years of rationalization and cover-ups? Will they not see me and everyone else partaking, and feel comfortable joining in regardless of their circumstances, as is largely the practice today that has led to all this weakness, sickness, and sleep in the body? Will they not only feel okay with it, but in addition feel the peer pressure to eat and drink when they may even feel they shouldn't? Will they then go forward to incur judgment, and this perhaps because of my conduct?

Is this then love, as I cause this weaker one to stumble? Do we see to our own comforts in the body and blood of the Lord, even as His bride continues on mired in weakness, sickness, and sleep? It pains me to not be able to partake in our modern observances, but I'd rather lose that privilege than help facilitate so many who now stumble because of the unworthy participation they foster. My solution is to partake within men's groups I'm involved in, where I know the issues involved and that we have discussed Matthew 5. Once that is done, I am no longer responsible for my brother's decisions, his judgement or his salvation. Such things are a matter between him and God.

Jane was a young lady who spent many years in our small group and was the kind of mature believer everyone looked up to. After she had attended several Communion ceremonies with us, she came to me one day concerned about her church because her pastor never proclaimed any of Paul's Communion warnings. I encouraged her to speak to him about it but she was afraid to confront him, so she chose the next best thing and began to just quietly abstain. Soon, God caused him to approach her to inquire as to why. She humbly explained to him her concerns about making others stumble. At first, he was offended and began defending his position. She came back to me with his arguments, we discussed them, looked at the scriptures, reinforced her resolve, and she stepped back into the fray.

Over time he came to acknowledge, albeit lukewarmly, her point and grudgingly began to read the entire account in 1st Corinthians when administering the elements! She rejoiced in the fact that her resolve to stand up for what she considered to be right would now result in her congregation at least being given an opportunity to hear the whole Word of God concerning the ceremony.

This story shows when we choose to abstain from the table because the admonishments are ignored, we can effect positive change in the way it is done. We can also be led into opportunities to evangelize or disciple those in the congregation who would ask us why—and some do ask why. I have seen the unsaved witnessed to when their believing friends abstained, and they asked why. I have also seen believers living in superficiality challenged when they asked why.

It is a truly odd occurrence in our day and age to see one who is an acknowledged disciple of Jesus abstain from the elements. Yet, I would submit that things would change if more believers understood the power, consequences, and promises involved in a reset table and abstained over concerns for weaker members in their somas.

Consider your ultimate mandate to make disciples who *observe all* Jesus taught. Consider your mandate to love and always put others before self, and God will bless it. Confront one another always in humility and love, as one who has struggles in life to another. Be diligent to follow up on your responsibilities as you bear another's burdens, God will see, and honor it.

Chapter IX

Ministering and Experiencing Admonishment

> "Nothing can be more cruel than the tenderness that consigns another to his sin. Nothing can be more compassionate than the severe rebuke that calls a brother back from the path of sin."
> — Dietrich Bonhoeffer

Jehovah Rapha gave us four basic ways, all of which need to be employed, to bring about His healing change in our lives:

- Yielding to the conviction of His Holy Spirit (John 16:8),
- Receiving the dissemination of His word (2 Tim 3:16-17),
- Prayer (Ps. 32:3-6) and,
- Interaction with other believers through confession (Jas. 5:16).

All are advanced in the message of Communion, but we must understand how to minister *and* receive them. Where repentance is concerned, the road to life with Christ for the seasoned disciple is the same as it is for the convert newly embracing salvation's call. Jesus, the mediator of grace and the Lamb of sacrifice, still stands before His children proclaiming, "Repent, for the kingdom of heaven is at hand!" When He preached this, He was calling us to change our minds and our course to the new kingdom He was bringing to earth, but also to turn from our former lives. The 'to' doesn't happen without the 'from,' and the 'from' without the 'to' leaves us without a roadmap to victory.

The church desperately needs to rediscover the art of ministering and receiving admonishment, a responsibility it relinquished to the "Christian therapists" long ago. Perhaps our best example of the process is found in Matthew 18. If an offender is unrepentant, actions proceed from correcting him privately, to taking two or three others along to establish the fact, to going to leadership with our concerns. If all else fails to bring about repentance, the church is to remove him from the fellowship.

Tough medicine, yes. But the Lord put these measures in place for a reason, designing the process to start quietly privately, and then slowly turning up the heat. Such actions have proven mild compared to the hell on earth to which we doom the unrepentant, along with the damage they can do to others, if we leave them alone in a state of self-delusion.

Bonhoeffer called it 'the cruelest tenderness'—of the Idol of Grace.

Jesus, ever our example, was not about to let Judas tarnish this special gathering at the Passover and thus removed him. Such discipline can and should be applied to the Communion setting, for intimate believers joined at the table is God's 'church' in its purest form. But it must be done in what Paul called 'a spirit of gentleness' (Gal. 6), especially where perhaps years of cover-ups participants may not want to face are coming to the surface.

The Communion setting, under Paul's order to examine ourselves and to strengthen the body, is tailor-made for entering into the process of ministering and experiencing admonishment: mano-a-mano and in small groups. Passivity here is not an option, for here is where the hypocrisy must end! This is not being mean-spirited or legalistic—no, it is the only hope for the self-deceived to turn from dangerous sinful practices. Inasmuch as they have rejected God's conviction, the fellowship needs to bring the message in a different form.

Under God's grace, there is always room for repentance, confession, and the fellowship to be re-established. However, such extreme measures are necessary sometimes or there would have been no need for Paul's warnings concerning unworthy participation in the Communion instruction, for Matthew to include the instruction for church discipline, or for Jesus to have manifested it at His Passover.

Again, I refer to Chambers in *My Utmost for His Highest*, agreeing with the need for the admonition Bonhoeffer and Paul speak to:

> If a person cannot go to God, it is because he has something secret which he does not intend to give up. He may admit his sin, but would no more give up that thing than he could fly under his own power. It is impossible to deal sympathetically with people like that…If you are sensitive to God's way, your message as His servant will be merciless and insistent, cutting to the very root. Otherwise, there will be no healing.

'Holy pressure' is absolutely necessary for a fruitful Communion experience. People are dying these days for constructive admonishment in their spiritual walks. They'll deny they need it, fight it, and try to avoid it. However, once pinned down and lovingly given no other path, the fruit typically comes forth and they come to embrace it! But how to receive and give it can be tricky.

Keeping it Balanced

I know much of what I write here may be hard to digest given its radical departure from what most have come to accept, and at this point your soul may be feeling a bit heavy. Breaking curses long embedded through denial and rationalization requires some shock treatment, but I have had to focus on the challenging aspects of Communion because that's the knife that is missing from the table and the power missing from the ceremony. But let us not forget John 13 and Proverbs 23 tell us it is because of 'the full extent of His *love*' that Jesus does not 'spare us the rod' of His admonishments, and also that Communion provides the perfect setting to engage in uncomfortable business in a setting of the love and care God has for each one of us.

We need to seek great discernment when dealing with admonishing, for we dare not overdo that aspect without constant reminders of the tender mercies of God's sacrifice at His table that brings things into balance. We must constantly keep in mind that, like Passovers without admonishments and disciplines has made the body weak, sick, and asleep, Passovers featuring too much admonishing can break spirits, promote condemnation, and become legalistic and Pharisaical. Jesus always displayed this balance of love and admonishment, and His Passover was no exception.

When He addressed most of the seven churches of the Revelation, He approached them with a message of, 'This I have for you...this I have against you.' As you both administer and receive admonishment, remember what God would have 'for us' and not just 'against us.' In the life of any believer, there exist both negatives we need help with and positives that should be cause for rejoicing. We should take some time to meditate on the good things God has done in our lives—areas where He has made us strong where we can help others—as well as areas where we are weak where another who is strong may step in and help us.

I could spend chapters discussing the identity issue but suffice it to say, 'Christ in us, the hope of glory' (Col. 1), and the fact that we are 'the righteousness of God in Christ' (2 Cor. 5) is pretty good news that should trump any of the struggles we may be having with our unwanted houseguest called the flesh. I believe The Lord's Table is here to set us free, not add burdens to existing struggles. However, that requires 'heaping heavy coals upon our heads' (Rom. 12) for a time. It will be Jesus' 'yoke that is light' participants will remember if we consider both the good and also to bring to light what is hiding in darkness. It's a time for the fellowship to come together in the name of freedom, not condemnation, so it's critical during times of administering and receiving admonishment we keep things balanced.

The Perfect Environment for a Chaotic Business

When we are caught in the webs of Satan's deceptions, we need true prophets who care more about our spiritual maturity than their popularity to speak into our lives. Brothers and sisters in Christ involving themselves in loving admonition is how dealing with sin, and in that process finding emotional healing, gets done. God knew the work of repentance can be a testy, uncomfortable business, and so provided Communion as a safe, yet effective, place for it to occur. It *requires* of everyone gathered an openness and vulnerability from which we are predisposed to shy away.

If we are to be led back from the malaise modern Christendom now finds itself in, it will be absolutely necessary that courageous administrators of the table, worthy of their trust and true to their ministry stand strong, love with tough love, and charge into the adversity self-exams always present! If they—if you—fail, the church will continue to waste this God-given golden opportunity to destroy immaturity and hypocrisy within her ranks. This is *the ceremony* where God provided a wonderful environment to enter in to the sometimes-testy business of speaking the truth to one another.

I again refer to Dietrich Bonhoeffer, whose passion for authentic Christian community I share. He wrote this concerning the importance of conviction within that environment in His book appropriately entitled, *Life Together* because holy life lived in community, under God's grace and instruction, is what Communion is all about:

> But God has put [His] Word into the mouth of men in order that it may be communicated to other men. When one person is struck by the Word, he speaks it to others. God has willed that we should seek and find His living Word in the witness of a brother—in the mouth of man.

Christ confronted His disciples through both His deeds and words at the Passover, as He broke from the gate there as never before with His own 'friends,' putting them on notice this would be a night where admonishments from the One *most* mature among them would be the process. Those who heard would either be ready to accept it or face a withering rebuke!

People engaged in coverups will need to hear from 'the mouth of a man' whom Christ has put in their lives to speak loudly because they refused to listen to His whispers. The wisest man who lived prior to Christ said, "Woe to the one who falls when there is not another to lift him up" (Eccles. 4). Solomon also said, "A friend loves at all times and a brother is born for adversity" (Prov. 17). The question isn't whether or not we will fall from time to time, it's will we have established close relationships with a brother or two who will be there to love us, charge into the adversity we are experiencing, and love us enough to get us back on track?

Recovery programs employ the concept of sponsorship and businesses employ mentoring, where one member who has matured through a growth process teams up with a newer one to help them walk a new and better path. Jesus sent His disciples out two-by-two, to face the challenges before them: encouraging, admonishing, and strengthening one another as He had done for them. The need for 'another man' is no different with Communion when it comes to a complete self-exam and, at the reset table with the knife employed, we find the perfect environment for it. As we should have learned by now, it doesn't happen in large church settings where the foxes are left in charge of their henhouses and little, if any, true self-reflection occurs.

Dr. Larry Crabb says this about a very real connection that takes place between believers when they both administer and experience proper doses of admonishment, discipline, and the balance of that within the environment of their fellowships:

> If the connection consists of profound acceptance, looking for the good, and the ability to see bad *without retreating*, then friendship exists in a relationship that can bear the weight of advice, rebuke, and failure and richly enjoy the pleasures of encouragement...If, however, the connection goes beyond acceptance to include penetrating wisdom and spiritual discernment, then friendship has deepened into shepherding.

Anyone who has tried to be God's vessel of admonition in the life of another has known the anxieties that emerge when wondering when and how to begin cutting through the cloak of self-deception, and at the same time keeping things encouraging and loving. It is even more intimidating for the one who is on the other end of it, trying to face God's hand of conviction upon him with integrity, perhaps for the first time. But if all is done in a biblical Communion environment, where administrators have opened the door and both parties have built a relationship of trust that will bear up under the strain, friendship can indeed 'deepen into shepherding.' But both parties must, in humility, courage, and love press into the process 'without retreating.'

Don't Disqualify Yourself

Finally, we must remember that God does not ask us to be perfect before confronting our brother. Rather, He has 'fashioned the body such that where one brother stumbles, another has been fashioned strongly' (1 Cor. 12). While we are all weak in certain areas, we are also all gifted with strength in other areas. Rather than bemoaning our shortcomings, let us focus on strengthening our brothers in areas where we are the more mature. It's not about being perfect—it's about the mandate of love that demands we come to the aid of our brother!

It is vitally important we 'do not retreat,' as Dr. Crabb says, during times of admonishing with the truth of the Word, because one of Satan's favorite diversions is having the confused play the 'you're judging me' card. He will do anything to deflect the truth from getting to those he has under his control, and he knows many Christians will flinch and avoid admonishing their brother thinking they're not perfect, so what right do they have to judge others? Stand firm despite your shortcomings, as we will see Paul and Peter did, and you will be a lifeboat in their seas of confusion.

If it were sin that kept us from speaking the truth in love, would we have any preachers of the Word? Any teachers?

Any ministers at all? The man who denied Christ three times in His hour of need went on to say, "But sanctify Christ as Lord in your hearts, *always* being ready to make a defense to everyone who asks you to give an account for the hope that is in you" (1 Pet. 3). After Peter's denial, Jesus didn't fire him and look for another first pastor of His church. He told Peter to go and strengthen his brothers once he had recovered. Furthermore, Paul didn't let the unwanted houseguest that dwelt in his flesh keep him from boldly proclaiming, "Be imitators of me as I also am of Christ Jesus" (1 Cor. 11)!

What perfect examples these two giants of the faith provide of grace working through sometimes flawed individuals! It matters not how weak or in what condition we may find ourselves [temporarily] under the weight of our own struggles, as long as we are not the ones engaged in covered-up sinful practices. ***Nothing, absolutely nothing, should keep one worthy participant at the table from lovingly and righteously coming alongside another brother in his hour of need with admonishment from the Lord.***

Christ Still Gets His Hands Dirty

Another lie that keeps many from experiencing anew God's admonishments is the idea that He can't forgive us again for the sins that seem to hang on over a long period of time. Darkness is allowed to live many times through the misguided notion that once Christ has initially climbed into the gutter of sin in our lives to save us, He refuses to sully Himself with our struggles thereafter. Rather than turning to Jesus to forgive our sins as we did when we got saved, and early on in our journey, we turn from Him in shame as a stubborn sin continues to haunt us.

This is not because Jesus refuses to forgive us '70 times 7,' it's typically because we refuse to forgive ourselves or believe He can continue to show us grace. Not that we are 'to sin all the more that grace may abound,' but if we are valiantly fighting and just struggling to find victory, we need to know He is still ready, willing, and able to put us back on our feet.

Does it occur to us that the One who sought out harlots and criminals, and returned to those who fled from Him in His hour of need to give them the keys to the kingdom of heaven, *was most effective when things were least attractive?* He was soiled most by our sin on the Cross of Calvary, yet He did His finest and most lasting work there. Jesus longs to get His fingers dirty in our lives if it comes as a result of genuine repentance that leads to action and spiritual growth. He longs to bring His light into our dark closets if it means we can 'remove the speck from our own eye so we can go help our brother' (Luke 6). He knows we're going to stumble in areas no matter how long we have been on this faith journey, and He never ceases 'living to make intercession for' (Heb. 7), and forgiving, the repentant.

The late Michael Wells was as close to a modern-day Paul as anyone you would ever know. He traveled the hellholes and backwaters of third-world countries around the globe much of the time to, in his words, "Bring the people Jesus."

Ministering and Experiencing Admonishment • 129

He only stopped when succumbing to one of the many exotic viruses he constantly battled due to his refusal to stop 'fighting the good fight and fulfilling his ministry.' God had given this man such simple yet profound wisdom due to the most obedient life lived I have ever witnessed, and I was honored to call myself his disciple. Michael said concerning getting up quickly when we stumble:

> As a believer, it is easy to turn one problem into five. You fall out with God before you fall into [sin]. Fall into condemnation and your problems will multiply. You must learn to get up as fast as you fall. Condemnation drives you from Him, where you will be sunk and move into angry rebellion.

Many times, the slow slide into the numbness of lawlessness starts when we believe Jesus couldn't forgive us again—for that same old *sin* again! Oh, how Jesus longs to forgive us—again—for that old thorn in our flesh as we approach Him with new humility, repentance, and willingness to get up as fast as we can and get back into the race! When a heart has stopped beating, it's time for courageous brothers to take out the defibrillator paddles and turn up the voltage! And that can't be done if we're wallowing in self-unforgiveness and pity.

Preach truth, love deeply, and show compassion but refuse to grant sympathy to people looking for it as a way to continue living in denial. When two or three gathered in His name are presented with the truth as they share the Word of God, the Spirit of God will reveal shortcomings and He will be there reveling in the maturing of His saints. This will ultimately lead to the peaceful fruit of righteousness coursing through the veins of everyone courageous enough to administer and experience admonishment.

Chapter X

The Best Confession

> Seeking what is true is not seeking what is desirable.
> — Albert Camus
> Therefore, when I admonish you to confession
> I am admonishing you to be a Christian.
> — Richard Renovare

We need to engage in 'the best' confession God affords because we are so adept at constructing cover-ups and rationalizations that create the very need for it. This is why it's so critical to provide an environment where confession in the fellowship of believers is promoted, expected, and, indeed, required. *If one understood why one was deceived one, by definition, would not be deceived. Without the help of others, it becomes impossible for the self-deceived, and therefore spiritually numb, to break out of paralyzing sin patterns.* Through protracted periods of disobedience and the numbness that ensues, they have come to think there is no need to be repentant because they truly believe nothing is wrong.

This is the essence of self-deception, and if the fellowship does not come together to help its deceived members pull out of the clouds and return to reality, they cease to be a biblical fellowship. Once again to the wisdom of Bonhoeffer:

> By sheer grace, God will not permit us to live even for a brief period in a dream world...A community which insists upon keeping its illusion when it should be shattered permanently loses in that moment the promise of... community. Sooner or later, it will collapse.

Those trapped in self-deception cannot help but weaken the body and confession is the key to shattering their illusions. If elders entrusted with the body's care allow weakness to remain, it can eventually cause effectiveness in the fellowship building itself up 'to collapse.' People can be present physically in a fellowship that has spiritually fallen down. Witness 'the church' today, with 90%+ of its members revealing they live in a 'dream world' within a religious system that 'insists upon keeping its illusion.' Is it any wonder her effectiveness at impacting a lost world is indeed collapsing, as record numbers are now ignoring or abandoning its edifices?

Communion is about setting up an environment conducive to confession, because without that an effective self-exam is, itself, an illusion. Without the help of mature mentors such people don't get better, don't even remain static, but they only get worse. Paul tells us, "Evil men will *proceed from bad to worse*, going out *deceiving and being deceived*" (2 Tim. 3). While most self-deceived people probably aren't evil, they are certainly listening to the voice of evil and not the voice of God, and the deceptions only deepen.

Our New Fig Leaf

The reason many fellowships hesitate to engage in the confessional process these days can be at least partly attributed to a dangerous element secular psychology has introduced into the church, and that concerns the concept that professionals alone can be entrusted with our deepest secrets because they will keep them 'confidential.' Before we discuss the benefits of biblical confession that heals the body of Christ, we need to look at this worldly counterfeit that keeps it from the unity it now lacks.

This dangerously exaggerated need for confidentiality has given many of the fallen Sons of Adam and Daughters of Eve new fig leaves to cover themselves with when the Spirit comes calling for confession. Don't believe it? Ask yourself why, when most small fellowship groups gather together and ask for prayer requests, members will only let others into the shallowest of the secrets? They'll allow prayer for physical ailments or friends or family in need but won't bring up the deep hurts that are doing the serious damage within their hearts and minds. Our serious requests will typically be deferred to anyone else who is hurting, but not us. While it makes people appear compassionate and loving, it's just a new fig leaf in the garden.

What are we to believe, when the day after our prayer meeting where they failed to speak of anything bothering them, people will go pay a therapist they barely know an excessive hourly wage to spill their guts? Why have Christian counselors become the church's new superstars, eclipsing even pastors when it comes to being respected for their advice? Why has Christian counseling become the accepted path to healing in the church while most fellowships struggle with intimacy and depth? Why do the numbers of students seeking counseling degrees from many of our seminaries now outnumber those seeking to be pastors and missionaries? I would say much of it revolves around this issue of seeking to hide behind confidentiality.

While there are certainly times when we must consider who to confess to under certain circumstances, and those who betray confidences should be admonished in our Communion celebrations as much as those who fail to confess, ***God never intended our sins to be confidential! It is the enemy who desires that.*** You cannot find a passage in the Bible that promotes keeping our sin to ourselves by hiding it from the fellowship.

The culture of confidentiality psychotherapy has brought into the church introduces a false light that allows us to believe we are confessing yet remain members that weaken the body. While a patient may confess their issues to their therapist, they know every time they gather for fellowship, they are continuing the cover-up with the very people they need to be closest to and, at the same time, robbing the fellowship of the opportunity to grow and mature. The cure for ineffective fellowships is to bring sin to the light and deal with it there, not keep it locked in a therapist's file cabinet.

The Bible speaks many times of 'two or three' gathered together in fellowship to confirm truth, invite Jesus into the picture, and provide love and admonishment. It does not speak of a patient huddled with a clinical professional outside of fellowship, or a priest in 'the confessional' to handle that responsibility. Therapists, both secular and Christian, are forbidden by professional mandate, with fines and legal consequences attached, to enter into anything resembling biblical fellowship with us. They cannot be our friends, embrace us with a holy kiss, or come over in the evening so we can pray or cry on their shoulders. Even moreso, they do not have the power of God for healing the fellowship that He does if we just engage, failing to function under the biblical prescription for healing set forth in James 5:16 [discussed fully in chapter 12].

So, would God command us to examine ourselves and confess sin, and then send us to an unbiblical setting to accomplish that? Would He not provide a way to expose what we found there to the light within His ecclesia once we had honored that command? By no means! He has given us the reset table for this precise purpose.

How was it that the believers in the Acts 2 church were 'all together' daily and 'had all things in common' if confidentiality is what they were seeking? Communion is the way God seeks us out in our hiding places, urges us to confess to that 'multitude of counselors' Solomon says will bring us victory (Prov. 11 & 24), and helps us stop hiding behind our fig leaves. To confess among our brothers and sisters in the body who are commanded by godly license [not forbidden by worldly license], to embrace us, love us, pray for us, bring accountability, and walk closely with us through to the end is the good wheat God wants to grow among us, not the chaff the enemy has planted through the blending of psychology and Christian counseling.

Jesus never kept quiet in the interest of confidentiality. He confronted people with their transgressions anywhere and everywhere, in public and in front of whoever was listening. Paul wrote letters to an entire church singling out one person who needed to be dealt with (1 Cor. 5). Was He worrying about confidentiality? In Galatians 2, He 'opposed Cephas [Peter] in the presence of all' for leading the Jews into hypocrisy. Jesus and Paul came to expose sin to the light and deal with it, which is perhaps why Jesus chose Paul to write the Communion instructions. They never allowed the targets of their admonishments the luxury of their fig leaves.

What this really comes down to is an issue of trust in both the fellowship and God Himself. Peter says, "Therefore, those also who suffer according to the will of God shall entrust their souls to a faithful Creator in doing what is right" (1 Pet. 4). During an effective Communion service, we will all 'suffer according to the will of God' when it comes to this issue of confession, because opening up our dark sin-closets to both Him and our brothers requires a certain amount of it. But we must trust in God to 'do what is right' with issues that make us uncomfortable, which He will do if we honor the table. His call is to confess our sins to 'one another,' and if that gets messy, we must trust Him that that's His will for us.

Healing is accomplished when two or more struggling saints who can say, "Been there – done that" get together in God's name for confession, prayer, a call to action, and the support and love to carry everyone through it. No degrees necessary, just a fellowship of people who understand what it means to be tempted themselves, so each might 'come to the aid of others who are also being tempted' (Heb. 2). We can run to the fig leaf of confidentiality, or we can run to the light. We have a choice: to hide behind professional confidences or trust in God and the fellowship. But if we desire biblical healing, there is only one selection.

Gossip

The damage gossiping can do, not only to the victims but to those who spread it, can be immense, and it is primarily due to loose lips the need for professional confidentiality has found a foothold in the church. When people are involved in cover-ups, sensitivity to this sort of thing is naturally very high and gossiping needs to be addressed. Discuss verses like Proverbs 13:3 and Romans 1:28-31 to help the group understand that those who hear confessions need to be mature and careful about spreading what they have heard beyond boundaries necessary for healing. The Again, two or more is a sufficient number to work out most of our important issues, for in those numbers 'every fact is confirmed' (Deut. 17, 19) and Christ promises to be present among us.

While all should be encouraged to trust the Lord and get over their fears of bringing their sins to light, if someone has heard a confession and thereafter wishes to seek more help to deal with the confessor or the problem, he or she should first gain the confessor's permission before sharing the issue with someone outside the immediate group brought into confidence.

The Good, the Better, and the Best

When I was a young boy, I used to love thumbing through my favorite department store catalog at Christmastime because it grouped individual gifts into 'good, better, and best' categories. Of course, my eyes would immediately wander to the 'best' first. Then, I would review the other two to see what it was that was 'best' about the best so I could formulate a devastatingly persuasive argument for my parents as to why I had to have that one. When it comes to the concept of self-examination Paul tells us is so critical to a rich and healing Communion experience there are good, better, and best ways to go about it. Why not employ 'the best?'

Is confessing to God alone the best way? Well, that may fit into the good or better categories, but is it the best? The halls of modern Christendom are littered with the immature who hid behind meaningless confessional prayers to God, thinking they were authentic. Confession to man alone is also a good thing, but could we call that the best? There is only one wise conclusion here, and that is if we want to avail ourselves of every weapon God has given us to fight the good fight of the faith against temptation and sin, confession both before God *and* man is the best way to go:

- Remembering Paul's instruction concerning seeking God's conviction in 1st Corinthians 4, the first inquiry where self-examination is concerned must go to the Lord.
- It then should proceed to a man examining himself, per Paul's Communion guidelines, to see if his assessment has been lining up with God's or if he has entered into the shadows of deception and cover-up.
- Finally, per James 5, we are to express our sins by 'confessing our sins to *one another* and praying for one another so that we may be healed.' God could

> heal us apart from confession to one another if He wanted to, but it would negate one of the primary reasons Jesus came, which was to model the power of love and unity in that all-important soma.

Look at the best confession, if you will, as a picture of the cross where we seek vertically for conviction and cleansing, and then horizontally for fellowship and healing. Either one without the other is an incomplete recipe. Observe Jesus' posture as He hung on His cross: He was looking up to His Father and reaching out in embrace to His bride—His community! Repentance [both *from* where we are and *to* where He wants to take us] and confession before both God and man is the cross of healing provided for us at the table, and this to maintain the spiritual readiness of His ecclesia and the individuals that comprise it.

In closing, a final comment from Dr. Crabb, the man who wrote the book on Christian therapy but then found a better way to be a catalyst of God's healing within the fellowship of believers, and why he observes that's not happening in the church:

> We no longer struggle together with our deepest concerns and our most internal battles...We rarely share in a way that requires the Gospel for the community to survive and for meaningful bonding to occur. The masks remain in place; we tell only of our stories, we deal [a bit proudly] with emotion-laden

struggles that don't disturb our final commitment to independence and we find ways to connect that don't require the depths of...grace.

If we offered more opportunities for brothers and sisters to gather in settings conducive to 'struggling with our deepest concerns and most internal battles,' there would be far more reality and depth in our relationships and a lot more healing in our fellowships. These settings were ordained in The Lord's Table, but we must move past ceremonies where 'the masks remain in place,'—beyond merely good or better and on to sharing in a way that requires the meaningful bonding of the Christian community to occur. This cannot help but bring about the unifying of God and the fellowship through divinely inspired purpose!

The goal of the Communion confessional is to find ways to connect that require the deepest depths of integrity, reality, grace, and love. This was the goal of the Writer of Acts as he exclaimed, "In view of this, I also do my best to maintain always a blameless conscience both before God *and* before men" (Acts 24). A blameless conscience is a healthy conscience that is maintained through the best confession during regular self-exams!

Chapter XI

Et tu, Judas?

> And if your hand causes you to stumble, cut it off
> — (Mark 9).
> I would rather be in a bad project with good partners than a good project with bad ones.
> — Jerrie Eckelberger

A message we need to seriously consider as we come to His Table is contained within Judas' seemingly normal life as a disciple, followed by his tragic betrayal, death, and everlasting legacy as the most infamous turncoat of all time. He and Pharaoh were unique players on the same stage, yet at different times in history. Each seemed predestined to suffer damnation to accomplish great exoduses for God's people. There is much to be learned from their mistakes within a discussion of Communion.

Once again, in Judas' dismissal Jesus set a living example of Paul's instructions as to how we need to fence the table properly. If there should be a Judas who causes stumbling in the fellowship, how that person needs to be subjected to church discipline [up to and including removal] can be found in Jesus' opening act at His Passover. It began with the words, "He who shares My bread has lifted up his heel against Me" (John 13).

To lift up one's heel against another means to injure them through employing deceit. When we partake unworthily in a table that honors truth and grace, don't we 'lift up our heel' against Jesus and the ecclesia by [as Paul says] 'sinning against the body and blood of the Lord?' As a result of Judas' own self-deception, his heart became closed to Jesus' influence and the door of his mind opened to the Father of Lies. I'm not suggesting we need to physically remove them. What I am saying is we resolutely admonish them to refrain from the elements and for them to use that time to reflect on why we did so.

When we allow such hypocritical 'clowns' to stay in the palace, we transform the table that is supposed to bring about freedom into an altar of judgment that invites the 'circus' of sin and self-deception to play on. Would Jesus have allowed an unrepentant Pharisee to join in His Passover meal? Paul would say in Judas' life weakness was revealed, sickness was exposed, and sleep [death] resulted. If we have allowed the light in us to become darkness through numbness to practiced sin patterns, and we stiffen our necks to the Spirit's persistent calls to repentance, God will allow us to seal our own fate. But that darkness must not be allowed to remain under the knife that was meant to surgically remove it! Jesus was not about to give the leaven of Judas any chance to spread to affect the rest of His apprentices.

I don't believe Judas was evil, as most seem to. Until that night when Satan 'entered in to him,' I think Judas was a confused follower not unlike so many in our church pews today. He seemed to be influenced by a group known as the Zealots [Barabbas' misled clan], insurrectionists who hated the Romans with a passion and viewed Israel as a kingdom-in-waiting, ready to return to prominence after they were defeated. The Zealot's image of the Messiah was of a warrior-king, leading His people to a glorious liberation of Israel. They thought they had found him when Jesus came riding into Jerusalem to thunderous applause, performing miracles, and speaking with the authority only the Messiah would be capable of. But He disappointed them when He rejected the role of king in favor of humble carpenter, itinerant preacher, and servant of all who came to willingly allow Rome to crucify Him.

I believe Judas' thinking on that Passover night could have gone something like this: "I have seen Jesus do things, and speak words, only the Messiah would be capable of and I know that many in power in Israel are, like me, looking for the promised liberator. So, if I can just mend the fences between Him and the leaders of the synagogue, perhaps we can all rise up and realize the goal of the glory of Israel. If the temple leaders can just come to appreciate Jesus as I do, and if He will just understand that if He combines His influence and abilities with those who control the human and financial resources within our faith, we can make it happen!" But Judas was wrong—dead wrong. Whatever his thinking, it had caused him to stray from the truth and nothing was going to change his mind.

No less than three times in Romans 1, Paul speaks of God 'giving over' stubborn, sinful people to their own desires which, in turn, leads to their destruction. When it came to this critical last night between Jesus and His disciples, the gig was up with Judas. Isn't it interesting that Judas' final fellowship with the disciples was at the place designated for self-exam and repentance? But when he would not repent, remaining intent upon carrying out his mislead plan, 'Jesus gave him over' to his deceptions and dismissed him 'with dispatch.'

Judas Not Unlike Us

While he eventually betrayed Jesus, it is clear that until the day this whole nasty scene unfolded in Jerusalem, Judas wasn't unlike any of the other disciples. Like all of them, he followed Jesus daily, went out to minister in His name when told to do so, sat at His feet to learn, and sometimes endured Jesus' unnerving rebukes. Without Judas' betrayal, would any of us read the Gospel's accounts of his actions and think of him any differently than the other eleven? Under that scenario, we could make a good argument that the intent of Judas to force this meeting was not for the sake of seeing Christ's ministry on earth terminated, but rather expanded.

And isn't it ironic that his act of betrayal did just that? Not that I wish to glorify Judas in any way, but even though everything went so wrong for him, his act of betrayal led to the explosion of Christ's ministry through His death and the coming of the Holy Spirit. Where once just the God-man indwelt with the Spirit did the work of the ministry, there were now twelve that would soon become hundreds and thousands likewise indwelt that one alone could never have reached!

If Judas were a secret-agent unbeliever whose mission in life was to see Jesus' ministry derailed, why then his comment to the temple leaders when he tried to return the coins that had purchased Jesus' death? Why such remorse as he cried, "I have betrayed innocent blood!?" Wouldn't he instead celebrate as he realized the success of his plan? Unless he truly believed in Jesus, why would Judas hang himself in despair as he came to understand, in one horrifying moment, that he had secured his legacy as history's most infamous traitor?

No, I think Judas was like so many today the polls tell us exalt Him 'with word and with tongue' and yet deny Him 'in deed and in truth' (1 John 3). And this is why it is vitally important to understand the scene that unfolded between Jesus and Judas at the Passover. Do we think for a moment that people trapped in destructive sin patterns, like Judas, pre-planned all of it looking forward to the day when they would face the Judgment Seat and possibly be 'cast into the outer darkness?'

Up until the point of his treachery, it seemed Judas wanted good things to happen to himself and others as a result of his influence. But then, somehow, he got off-course. Like Judas, can't one misconception of the truth or piece of accumulated baggage cause us to make bad choices when we think we are doing right? Eventually our small and seemingly insignificant wrongs snowball into an avalanche of bad decisions and collateral damage.

How many people get to the end of their lives, once so full of dreams and hopes like Judas, wondering where it all went so wrong? None of us plans to fail. None of us intend to make small mistakes that turn into huge issues that ruin our lives, but it happens all the time.

Has The Enemy Entered In?

The Bible tells us the reason Judas did his evil deed was because 'Satan entered into him.' As discussed earlier, while the institutional church largely ignores the issue and many naïve Christians believe Satan can't touch us after conversion, deliverance ministers know that he can and does 'oppress us' through demonic means (Acts 10:38). This oppression comes through permissions we grant them via our own activities, or the activities of others perpetrated upon us. Paul lamented over engaging in the very practices he hated, saying, "I find then the principle that *evil is present in me*, the one who wishes to do good" (Rom. 7). Can any of us, therefore, honestly say we are immune to the deceptions of the mind and demonic influences of the enemy that brought about Judas' downfall?

While I do acknowledge that his was a very unique case, I also know that many who believe in Jesus share in his self-delusion. Otherwise, what would have led Paul to so clearly warn the Corinthians of the grave consequences for improperly partaking of the elements, even back then when the church was young and the Spirit so alive? Judas no doubt said, "Lord, Lord" many times, but did this deed born of deception anyway.

I wonder, as I look upon the state of modern Christendom, if Jesus does not pose the question to many who call Him Lord that He asked of Judas: "Do you betray the Son of Man with a kiss?" Would He ask, as Julius Caesar did of his good friend Marcus Brutus when he was stabbed to death by him and others who feigned allegiance, "Et tu [you too], My child?"

Tragically, such betrayals happen all too often in modern-day Communion services. People tell Him how much they love Him while harboring unconfessed sin and living superficial lives. But this is because most people lack a proper understanding of Communion's glorious purpose and not because of Judas' disease, and so I write this in the hope what we see today springs from improper observances held over decades of most people's church lives—in the hopes that proper teaching and modeling of biblically-observed Communion can and will make a difference.

Judas thought he could mold Jesus into his own image of what he thought the Messiah should look like, and it cost him his eternal soul. How many today think they can mold Jesus into a god who blesses their habitual sin addictions because they participate in meaningless repetitions of religious church rituals? How many modern Judases will get to the end and find out they have sold their souls for a bag of silver?

After it's too late, how many will desire to go back and change how life turned out, like he did? How many will have spent a lifetime saying, "Lord, did we not…?" only to hear Him respond, "Depart from Me, I never knew you" (Matt. 7)? According to Jesus, many more will go that way than will find 'the narrow gate that leads to life.'

"*Et tu*, Judas?" This is a question none of us wants to hear at Christ's judgment seat. Learn from his example now and don't let small, poor choices mature into a practiced lifestyle of lawlessness. Join in the joys and responsibilities of regularly celebrating the Lamb of Sacrifice, and let Judas remain his own singular, pitiful legacy.

Chapter XII

The James 5 Gathering

> You see, for forgiveness to be effected,
> there must first of all be confession of sins.
> — Tegume Thomas

The practical application of the self-examination process comes forth primarily through two activities. While I have alluded to these philosophically, their practical application within the Communion environment makes them the two-edged sword—the 'knife'—God intended to surgically extract and bring to light buried issues that hinder us. Accomplished within a setting of tough love, sincere repentance, humility, prayer, and loving admonition, they make all the difference in a fruitful Communion ceremony. All worship and teaching has been to prepare souls for this moment. The group must now come together at a table reset to see to it that none who claim Christ fail this crucible so critical to fruitful self-examinations, thus accomplishing the goal of restoration and healing God desires.

Participants must now unite as a body because the truth from God is often times 'found in the mouth of a man' and can, and most often does, 'burn all the way down.' It is a necessary hurt, a glorious hurt, a healing hurt, and a sanctifying hurt, but painful nonetheless. Just as our journey to the kingdom must begin with the first of the nine words that changed everything ["repent for the kingdom of heaven is at hand"], so also during this process the journey to healing must begin with confession of sins before both God and man.

The Vertical Confession Process

Remembering Paul's words in 1st Corinthians 4, the first confession we must engage in is *vertical*, coming humbly before the throne of God to proactively seek His conviction of sin through individual prayer. We must pass no judgments on ourselves or others before we do, for apart from Him, no judgment would carry true wisdom and godly insight with it. Furthermore, once this step is undertaken those struggling will be more inclined to acknowledge that and seek help.

Once the Spirit has passed judgment and disclosed to the individual participants the true nature of their sin, the fellowship can begin to judge itself individually and collectively, and act according to His will. It is through this time of proactively seeking God's conviction that the Holy Spirit will bring those issues we are, per Matthew 5, to 'here remember' into the open. This is a time to remember the Lord's request we 'reason together' discussed earlier so that we may not be judged, but that our sins be washed away.

The group should be broken up so that each individual can quietly find a place to be alone with God. In the quiet of their time, all should be encouraged to reflect upon passages such as 1st Corinthians 4, Philippians 4:6-7, 1 John 1:9, Psalm 139:23-24, and others included on the Prayer Recorder [see Appendix B] at the end of this book. Make copies and hand them out to everyone before they go out. Space to record anything God leads them to 'there remember' is found on the recorder.

This is not a time for intercession for others, for worship, or for general prayers of any kind. The believer walking in denial and cover-ups typically has, and will continue if allowed, to use such prayers to avoid the necessary surgery in their own closets by deflecting to other, less painful topics. What it is a time for is to confess known sin to God, but more importantly, to ask Him to identify any hidden motivations of the heart (1 Cor. 4:5) that lead us to do what we do. Here we ask the Holy Spirit to honor His promise to have us 'here remember' the issues that are imprisoning us, and then quietly and intently listen to what He says.

Once that connection has been made, participants need to use the Prayer Recorder to make a list of all persons [including God Himself] He reveals who may 'have something against them' and why, along with anything else the Spirit prompts them to record. If you will but courageously ask, I promise you God will reveal to you everything you need to understand about your transgressions and what you need to do to deal with them because, again, this is the very place He ordained for it. He will bring to your remembrance all admonishments He wants you to consider, and the love He wants you to embrace, as Jesus did with the disciples at His Passover.

We all fear the consequences of this kind of invitation to the truth, but it's such a silly anxiousness when we consider Jesus already knows every dark thought and every dark deed we have had or done. We are merely inviting Him to show us that which He already longs to reveal! Journaling any thoughts that come to mind during this time on the Prayer Recorder will help everyone focus on what's truly important and provide a future personal prayer and action list for each participant during confession time and beyond [**note: for those sincere in their quest, there is no irrelevant thought here! Whatever participants hear, no matter how strange it may seem, it needs to be recorded.** The input of the fellowship can help clarify any confusing thoughts].

As participants enter into this time of confession, any conviction that remains unattended to keeps us that much further from the healing Jesus desires we accomplish 'round the table. This is the ordained time to let all the ugliness that is within be exposed so it can come out, and to offer up heartfelt pleas to our gracious God for His mercy that waits in abundance! Encourage renewed belief and trust in that body broken, and blood of the New Covenant of grace and mercy poured out, as all wrestle with the Spirit Who must first wound to heal.

James 5: The Horizontal Confession

Having returned from prayer, the discussion can begin for the second step—the one that this Passover setting was tailor-made for, yet one I have *never* seen observed in modern church observances. What I call The James 5 Gathering is the one that represents the difference between merely attending Communion and genuinely participating. Would the Spirit disclose those issues He wants us to remember, and then leave us on our own to deal with them? Horizontal confession and prayer, following its vertical counterpart, opens the door to complete the Holy Spirit's needed surgery and bring about profound healing through 'the soma' if we will but have the faith and courage to engage.

This is confession before the brethren: the critical ingredient to making the experience all that God intends: 'admitting to another human being the *exact* nature of our struggles.' *Examining oneself—one of the two prime directives of the ceremony—cannot be experienced fully or effectively without it. This is the uncomfortable 'knife' intended to cut deeply and do real surgery, and at the same time the process that honors and strengthens the body.* It's time to let this Big Dog of conviction hunt as He runs wild through the fellowship!

Therapists, psychologists, and counselors have made a billion-dollar business out of realizing that hurting people need to confess and come clean. What a concept! If only the church, where the idea came from in the first place, understood and employed it. This is to be a time to take the Prayer Recorder and confess the *exact* nature of our own personal struggles with sin to at least one other [preferably more] human being. Generalizations and evasions here might soften the blow for the moment, but they will only allow continued patterns of superficial living and prolonged suffering, so leadership must keep a firm hand on the rudder now more than any other time.

The time of small-group confession is not just a time for the hurting to unburden themselves, but also a time for those hearing confessions to revel in their mission of reconciliation and write down any burdens of the confessee they should help bear (Gal. 6). This may mean service, a commitment to pray for someone, intervene in a dispute, hold someone accountable to a Communion commitment, or just to come quietly alongside them in their hour of need to listen.

Confession exists as much for the good of the confessed-to as for the confessee. This is a rich time for participants to share the *'rhema'* [spoken] word of God together—time to find wisdom 'in the mouth of a man.' Many times, if we listen both to God and our brother as he is making a confession, the Spirit will speak to us with a word for him. There is no opportunity better than right here, right now, for those gathered to speak the Rhema Word into one another's lives.

James 5 says, "Is anyone among you sick? Let him call for the elders of the church and let them pray over him." It is critical, once a confession is made, that others receiving it pray on the spot for the confessee. James continues, "And the prayer offered in faith will restore the one who is sick, and the Lord will raise him up. And if he has committed sins, they will be forgiven him." James then says, "The effective prayer of a righteous man can accomplish much." When men made righteous in Jesus and the Holy Spirit engage in their Communion responsibilities, while the hurting and confused do theirs, the fireworks happen!

There is no hiding here—nowhere to run. When confession, one to another, is employed after earnestly seeking God's conviction within the environment He ordained for self-examination, the floodgates of the living water of the Spirit burst forth in a kaleidoscope of emotion, relief, self-revelation, and cleansing of the soul! This is true for those confessing, for those forgiving and praying with them, and for those who respond by fulfilling their responsibilities to Christ's one and only law to 'Bear one another's burdens' during the times between Communion celebrations.

James concludes this passage as he speaks to the reward for faithful administrators of the table, "My brethren, if any among you strays from the truth and one turns him back, let him know that he who turns a sinner from the error of his way will save his soul from death, and will cover a multitude of sins." For those confessing and ministers alike, it *all* works for *everyone* involved when we honor the process by bringing sin into the light.

To summarize the effectiveness of Jame's message, confession:

- Forces us to humble ourselves: This is a vital process in the life of the growing saint. Superficial façades cannot be upheld when confessing sin face-to-face. Pride of spirit disintegrates in the light of confession in the flesh.
- Brings sin out into the light: We as believers were created to deal with our sin before God and within the fellowship, to take cover-ups out of the darkness where they thrive and into the light where they die. Anyone who hasn't known the liberating, freeing experience of fully exposing their sin to the light of fellowship is living under a burden none of us was intended to bear. The yoke of unreconciled sin never stops, never sleeps, and never takes a holiday until it is dealt with.
- Brings about accountability: Accountability, while not the ultimate solution, can be a great means to an end. When our sin is in the open, our brothers and sisters can help us check on our progress—a process that strengthens both parties to the confessional.

- Ensures true fellowship: Paul tells us that fellowship refreshes our spirit by helping us understand we are not alone in our weaknesses. Where secret closets of unconfessed sin exist, true fellowship cannot.
- Establishes a valuable practice of experiencing and participating in brotherly love: Participating in biblical, mano-a-mano, confession will make it easier for the members of your fellowship to fully participate whenever 'two or more come together.'
- Provides encouragement: The Writer of Hebrews urged the church to consider how to stimulate and encourage all to love and good deeds (Heb. 10). How many times are we encouraged by a word from our brother or sister when it seems God's voice has been silent? ***We won't find the love of God in God alone. The Great Commandment has two intertwined elements, not just one, because love requires both a source and a target.*** Love and the encouragement it brings is not stagnant and must flow to exist.

At the risk of being redundant, I cannot stress strongly enough that the circle of self-deception leading to superficiality and hypocrisy comes through extended periods of unconfessed, unrepentant, unchallenged disobedience to God, and the isolation from the fellowship resulting, that then becomes a practice. This typically involves years where gatherings have been shallow and non-confrontational rather than effective. It leaves people feeling numb and disconnected.

Putting Feet To Repentance

Robert came to me during a Communion confessional and said the Spirit had been constantly having him 'there remember' an experience that, up to that night, he had all but forgotten. He had damaged a fence with his car speeding out of his high school parking lot some years earlier when he lost control in the gravel on the shoulder of the road. Suddenly, after years of burying the memory, it was all he could think of that night. I reminded him of Matthew 5, suggested it was obviously something God wanted him to deal with, and encouraged him to be attentive to the Spirit's promptings. He replied, "Guess I've got to go and make things right."

Some days later, he called me and told me he had gone to the owner of the fence, told him what had happened, asked his forgiveness, and said that he wanted to make restitution. The owner was amazed at this young man's honesty, for the fence had been damaged many times by other students over the years and yet Robert had been the only one to fess up. The man gathered his entire family in the living room to talk to Robert! He was presented an opportunity to share the gospel with them, all because he honored the table and put feet on his repentance. This was The Matthew 5 Alternative in action, and repentance 'in deed and in truth!'

In 2 Kings, chapters 22 and 23, we find a story about an amazing king and man of God—one that magnificently illustrates the concept of participatory repentance, the

Passover it engendered, and its effect on an entire nation. We are told, "King Josiah did right in the sight of the Lord." While there were many good kings found in the books of the Kings, even those who did some good things left out one critical act in the repentance process: tearing down the high places where sacrifices were made to pagan gods. This angered Jehovah greatly, and He communicated as much to Josiah in response to his prayers.

But, unlike his predecessors, Josiah decided to act. As the story in chapter 23 plays out, he deals in no uncertain terms with all the false gods, their idols, their prophets, and their high places. These actions—this participatory repentance unlike any of the kings before him—caused the following to be written of Josiah: "And before him there was no king like him who turned to the Lord with all his heart, and with all his soul, and with all his might according to all the law of Moses. Nor did any like him arise after him." Think about it! This puts Josiah in rarefied air with King David: 'the man after God's own heart!'

What is germane to our discussion is what happened next: "Then the king commanded all the people saying, "'Celebrate the Passover to the Lord your God as it is written in this book of the covenant.' Surely such a Passover had not been celebrated from the days of the judges who judged Israel, nor in all the days of the kings of Israel, and of the kings of Judah."

Did Josiah just come up with the idea to celebrate the Passover after his proactive repentance? No, for at long last the stage had been properly set for the Passover God had intended due to repentance in deeds as well as in words! It was only after the actions of repentance that God put in Josiah's heart to institute the Passover once again. The table had finally been properly set by a courageous shepherd willing to yield the knife and a people who had turned their hearts and minds back to God because of it. Not even in the golden age of Israel, when David and Solomon reigned, had there been such a Passover celebrated!

This story shows us that we, too, can celebrate Communion such as we have never celebrated, where putting feet on our repentance causes us to connect with our heavenly Father and our fellowship as never before. When sin has lost all its power and is no longer able to tear the fellowship apart, true communion between the lost sheep and the brethren, and the lost sheep and God, is restored in a glorious reunion made possible through this magnificent ceremony!

How It Looks

Shoe-leather repentance can take on many forms, from the simple to the extremely delicate and complex. But simple or complex, it is never easy. Many times, it's just a matter of personal sin where others aren't involved, or they are and would readily understand and accept the making of amends. However, there are times when we would do more harm than good in confronting certain people who have been involved in our transgression. Without proper discernment and wisdom, we can dig up buried skeletons of a type that would cause others to suffer while trying to heal ourselves. This violates all biblical notions of love and the intent and spirit of Matthew 5.

If such a case exists, we could find someone who may know both parties involved or may be aware of the situation and confess it to them. That person could then do whatever the effective follow-up would mandate without causing harm. Within the confines of Communion, a perfect opportunity exists to get input from others concerning what the right thing to do would be in making the path of repentance a wise and loving one.

Another obstacle can involve pure logistics. Many times, we may find ourselves in a position during a Communion service where personal contact with those we need to mend fences with just isn't possible. While Matthew 5 is to be taken seriously, needlessly crucifying ourselves over past mistakes that we cannot go back and right is fruitless. In this case, let confession to others in the body be the action and leave it there. God will see, hear, and honor sincere attempts to repent and confess. Always use discretion and pray about whom you wish to confess to, what circumstances He wants you to deal with, and how.

As always, if you need help in understanding certain situations remember Solomon's words in Proverbs 11: "In an abundance of counselors there is victory." The Holy Spirit, who indwells all gathered, will provide the right person for every confession and discernment in each situation when we honor the ceremony by being obedient to our best understanding and ability. Furthermore, while Matthew 5 makes it clear that we need to come to the altar *after* repairing damaged relationships with those who have something against us, I believe a sincere verbal and personal commitment to those gathered 'round is enough to allow one to partake—*once*. If the table is fenced properly and an environment of reverence established, you won't need to impress upon the confessee the seriousness of his or her Communion commitment before God and the body.

If the commitment to do whatever it takes to proactively follow through and begin anew in a growing relationship with Christ is made, and that commitment is verbalized, then participation in the elements should be encouraged. Due to Communion being observed regularly, a commitment made that is made and not acted upon can come up again at the next observance. However, this time the knife needs to be employed, and that person will need to be instructed to abstain from the elements until real action is taken, inasmuch as their earlier commitment was superficial.

Superficiality always results when people think mere words suffice where actions are necessary. They cannot escape their obligations to act when Communion, properly administered, doesn't allow it. Behold 'the knife' and the practical, functional beauty of restoring the balance of truth and grace!

Chapter XII

Baby Steps

While for many it will be hard initially to take on everything they know they need to bring to light, they must, at a minimum, be willing to start working on what God has had them write on the Prayer Recorder list. Encourage baby steps, but steps nonetheless, so the process does not overwhelm them. What is important is opening lines of communication with God that sin have closed and proceeding towards an understanding of genuine repentance, action, and positive movement toward the goal of total healing.

Practiced sin patterns are formed over extended periods of time, and demanding the road out be short and immediate can crush spirits, destroy trust, and damage any progress that may otherwise be accomplished. What some would consider baby steps may, for others, be huge leaps of faith! If it is evident this message has been understood, they will be on their way to taking advantage of the opportunities presented to them at later observances.

God won't let those humbly participating be burdened beyond what they are able. We need to be a part of what the One who best knows what His flock can handle wants done. All need to listen to His Spirit and make efforts to act depending upon, but not exceeding, the urgency of His promptings.

Pray for wisdom for all to know when to press and when to back off. Pray for spiritual discernment among the flock, especially for your Communion administrator. Pray for a spirit of tough love and compassion that will be evident to all during this time. The reset table is a place where the fellowship fulfills the law of Christ by bearing upon its broad shoulders the burdens its weaker members have been unable to bear alone.

No Promises

Concerning follow-through with our Communion business, the Bible warns us about making promises of any kind. Jesus warned that we were to make *no oaths at all* but to let our statement be a simple 'yes' or 'no.' Anything beyond this, He said, would be 'evil' (Matt. 5). James echoed this admonishment and forewarned we would fall under God's just judgment if we made promises (Jas. 5). Even in the Old Testament, where promise-making was encouraged under the law, God warned, "Pay what you vow! It is better that you should not vow than that you should vow and not pay. Do not let your speech cause you to sin." (Eccl. 5).

We make our 'wedding vows' [words found nowhere in the Bible] and half of Christian marriages now end up in divorce. Promise-making changed under the New Covenant because God knew we would struggle keeping them, and that failing to do so was one of the reasons the former covenant didn't work. We are to let our deeds speak louder than our words if we want to display true integrity. Communion is to be about changing who we truly are rather than continuing to live in a superficial, disconnected reality.

Therefore, when it concerns necessary actions brought to light at the table, simply make the commitment to yourself, and then verbalize it to God and the fellowship by saying something like, "With God's help, I will do my best to..." Or, "I now know I need to..." and then let your yes be yes by acting on that commitment. Promises made and then not kept become lies, and lying is a sin. Not only that, it is lying to ourselves that fosters self-deception and hypocrisy to begin with. Refuse to ask for, or give any oaths concerning, what you or anyone else will or will not do. If another participant is into making promises, remind them of Jesus' and James' words, encouraging them to just go do whatever it is they were going to promise to do. The purpose of making a Communion commitment is to derail sin patterns, not engage in new ones.

Finally, the administrator needs to stress at this point if anyone will not confess and at least begin the process of proactive repentance regarding one or more of the issues God had them 'here remember,' abstinence is the only safe course. This is not legalistic—it's tough love and the administrator must stand strong against any accusations that it is. Such arguments will come through someone using them as a defense, which they have no-doubt become very adept at.

The buck of rationalized and denied sin stops here at The Communion table, because here is where God ordained it to stop! Communion was masterfully crafted to shatter walls of denial and hypocrisy, not enforce them.

This is a part of the self-examination process that simply must be engaged and then pressed through regardless of any temporary discomfort. Be strong and of good courage. Stay the course, employ both the rod and the staff God has given you in love, and destroy the deceptions of the enemy!

Chapter XIII

Walking Through a Powerful Ceremony

"We have all the light we need.
We just need to put it in practice."
— Albert Pike

Now that we've discussed the individual elements of the reset table, let's put it all together in summary. To begin, we simply must change the physical environment we now employ. Members of the church in Acts 2 gathered day-by-day in the temple but partook of Communion 'house to house.' This method corresponds perfectly with Jesus' Passover, as at the time, He was 'teaching daily in the temple (Luke 19)' in Jerusalem, but specifically selected the more intimate and private setting of a home for His observance. It is simply not possible to accomplish what He accomplished there, or what Paul tells us we must accomplish today, in a typical church service or other large group settings.

I believe Jesus knew that in such settings, where both believers and unbelievers would be in attendance, it would be impossible for administrators to properly facilitate the wielding of the knife so healing could occur. He also knew that people trapped in self-deceptive webs of sin would prefer to remain anonymous in large crowds where they could continue to hide while feeling like they weren't. Brian Hathaway discusses what his church discovered concerning the proper environment for Communion in his insightful model for building a Christ-centered fellowship:

> One of the stumbling blocks for us in the breaking of bread service had been the linking of worship and Communion in the same service. *There is no Biblical precedent for this.* By separating these two activities it is possible to be much more flexible. We encourage people nowadays to take Communion together in home groups...*It was birthed in relationships, and should be practiced in relationships.* [Italics mine]

One of the many things Jesus came to give us was a new definition of the word 'family,' and it was with His new spiritual family alone that He partook of His Passover. There, in the Passover of the Exodus, and the home churches established by the Holy Spirit, we see a completely consistent biblical Communion model of 'family' coming together in an intimate setting. As with all other things He made new, Jesus restored the Passover to its proper environment after religion had done what it always does to faith, by making it comfortable and structured, numbing it down to nullify its effectiveness.

Establishing an Environment

Considering the usual spontaneity of Jesus during His ministry, the meticulous preparations made at His behest for the Passover seem rather odd. He typically preached from boats, in fields, and on mountaintops, inviting Himself to eat with anyone and everyone at a moment's notice. True to His claim, He Himself was a man who 'had nowhere to lay His head' (Luke 9). Uniquely at His Passover do we ever find Jesus preparing an environment of any kind.

Churches across America prepare meticulously for services every Sunday. Great pains are taken, and copious amounts of money spent, to make sure the worship music, lighting, sound, audio-visual presentations, message, and all the various trappings of the sanctuary are as impressive as they can possibly afford. *If we so meticulously prepare for services that Jesus was totally spontaneous about, what kind of effort should we expend to prepare for a ceremony He was so meticulous about?* Below are a few suggestions to help in arranging your 'upper room':

- Location: Gather at a neutral place or the home of the administrator. If it is the home of another in the group, they may be tempted to focus more on hosting than in participating and will be overly concerned with what people think about their property. I recommend a 'getaway' kind of place that has numerous small areas of privacy where small groups can gather together for confession and prayer. This can be a borrowed cabin, a small conference center, or—weather permitting—a campsite or other outdoor location away from crowds.

Weekend retreats are ideal. They present the opportunity to spend Friday evening and Saturday teaching and fully experiencing prayer and confession, with the elements taken Sunday morning. This provides a superb atmosphere for fellowship and gives people extra time to chew on what the Spirit is trying to accomplish in them.

Computers, cell phones, and other distractions should be left in a room away from the ceremony. Allow one phone in the ceremony for emergencies, but that is all. Get rid of any and all possible distractions, as Jesus did the night of His Passover. Distractions have been the order of the day for those who want to avoid getting to the heart of their problems, and the enemy will employ as many of them as you allow to be present.

- Drive-time fellowship: A drive of an hour or so to the location is a great way to spur conversation and establish a natural state of fellowship. Carpooling provides a great opportunity to bring people together where they can begin to interact within a critical social mass.

- What to bring: Aside from those necessities involved in an overnight trip [if that's what you decide], only Bibles, a guitar, and the Communion elements should be included. As Paul instructed the Corinthians, everyone should be well-fed beforehand, so perhaps you can stop and dine on the way to your destination which will further enhance fellowship.
- Childcare: Children and babies need to be left with friends or family. If you have other small groups in your church, perhaps form teams that help each other with childcare. Inasmuch as I recommend keeping the sexes separate for numerous reasons, hopefully husbands can watch the kids for wives and vice versa. Let young people join with others of their peers for their own reset table. This book was developed within a youth group setting where teenagers more readily adapt to changes that challenge traditional thinking.
- Group size and makeup: I have found a group of eight to twelve to be ideal for this. If you have too few, some may feel you have failed to reach a critical mass. And to them, this is important. Too many, on the other hand, will be difficult to shepherd, possibly allowing those in denial to hide in the crowd.
- Time: Give plenty of time. When the Spirit moves as He will here, time must be granted and control released to Him. Hurting and superficial people

need to be given time to deal with their issues, both before their brethren and God. Within reason, time needs to be allowed for the kind of individual prayer, confession, and fellowship that is critical to an effective self-examination/healing process. Do not attempt to muzzle this Ox when He's on His threshing floor!

- Frequency: I recommend employing this in-depth ceremony two to three times per year. It should be special and looked forward to with anticipation by the participants. Even though done infrequently, you will find an amazing thing will happen when a reset table is fully experienced and understood within the small group setting: regular Communion services 'at church' will take on new meaning and significance. People will understand why observing it in remembrance of Jesus—*all of Him* and not just grace—is so vitally important.

The Ceremony

Once the ceremony has begun, here are some suggestions for enhancing its effectiveness. Considering the enemy's plan to turn faith into religion by over-structuring it, and yet also Jesus' meticulousness in preparing for His Passover, administrators need to seek balance here:

- Opening Worship: In the Passover accounts in Matthew, Mark, and Luke, Jesus set the tone by singing a hymn with His disciples. Begin your time with a prayer from the small-group leader that begins challenging participants from the outset, then worship to set the spiritual tone. While prayers should never be canned, the themes we've discussed to this point need to be maintained throughout by leaders on a mission to unleash Communion's power and see results. Worship songs or hymns should be focused on God: reverent and simple with no complicated melody lines or lyrics that are hard to follow. If necessary, word sheets should be easily readable with large print. The ideal environment for worship facilitates a total focus upon God, with nothing else to distract.
- Washing feet: In the Gospel account of John, one of the first things Jesus did was to wash the feet of the disciples to show them they were not to be masters but servants of one another. He then said they should do likewise. This can be a wonderful way to relieve tensions new and different ideas always cause and begin opening hearts to a radically different ceremony. The group's leader can ask one person to come forward, wash that person's feet and say something edifying about or to them. Then, invite someone else to take a shot at it with another they wish to lift up. Hopefully, this will become contagious 'round the

table. If nothing else, it will establish the administrator as one unafraid to blaze new trails and strive to make the ceremony all it can be.

Teaching: If Jesus found it so important to present all we read in John 13-16 at His Passover, and Paul found it so important to teach specifically on the subject to the Corinthians, shouldn't we give thought to exact teaching during Communion services as well? Again, Peter forewarned that people forget important truths and so reminders are good (2 Pet. 1). The master deceiver is relentless in his attempts to put us to sleep to our sin. Therefore, the teaching needs to be done *every time*, even if abbreviated because everyone in the group has heard it before, to 'stir up their spirits by way of reminder' and prepare them for that new thing God is always doing.

Leaders will find an outline at the end of this chapter they can copy and use. Teach, of course, as the Spirit leads but try to include most of the subjects on the outline. Of utmost importance is that everyone understands the concept of proactively seeking God's conviction in prayer, the interactive healing confession of the saints, repentance through both words *and* deeds, and the opportunity given us in Matthew 5.

- Prayer [vertical examination]: After the teaching remind everyone they will, from this point on, 'be standing on holy ground.' Hand out the Prayer

Recorders you have hopefully made copies of [or at the very least paper and pens] and split up the group for about thirty minutes to allow time for their Holy-Spirit exam. Suggest participants read the verses on the Recorder and write down all that comes to their minds no matter how trivial, irrelevant, or strange it may seem. Remind them also of Matthew 5, and that *here* is the place the Holy Spirit will bring them to remember all the kingdom business that He wants them to attend to if they sincerely invite Him in.

- Small-group confession [horizontal examination]: After calling participants back from prayer, talk about the power of James 5:16. Then split everyone into smaller groups and grant plenty of time to allow participants to confess the items they've written down to others and to receive counsel and intercessory prayer. Tell them to feel free to move around from group to group as the Spirit leads, as long as they are not doing so to avoid confessing. Instruct them the confessional needs to be done in a spirit of both love and reverence, to keep focused on what they have just heard from God in prayer, and to seek the power to carry out any tasks He has placed before them. Solemnly remind all gathered that if there is anything God had them write on their Prayer Recorders they can't bring themselves to confess to at least one other person, it indicates cover-ups. Also remind them if they can't find the courage to

at least confess and begin working on a few of them, they need to seriously consider abstaining from the elements.
- The end gathering: After sufficient time has been given for the confessional process, call the group back together to partake of the elements [unless it is an overnight stay or weekend retreat, in which case I would suggest waiting until after breakfast the last morning to give additional time for self-reflection]. Some confessional groups may have to be cut short, but encouragement can be given to them to continue at a later time. Once more, stress that there are real consequences for partaking unworthily and that you, as their shepherd who loves them, would hate to see any in your care go on suffering needlessly on your watch. Remind them also that Matthew 5 is the way to safely proceed if they have any questions at all concerning their thoughts and conduct. At the table ordained to restore holiness, it is better to be safe than sorry. *We will never be condemned for abstaining in the interest of coming back later in victory. We will always be judged for partaking unworthily.*
- Finally, admonish all that every participant's decision made in honesty and humility should be a cause for rejoicing—whether it be to partake or abstain. For those who feel the Spirit is prompting them to let the elements pass at this time, the goal is to share

the victory of Matthew 5 the next time you gather. For those who know they have done all to be found worthy, they can rejoice in a healthy maintenance checkup successfully completed! Remind everyone of their obligation to 'bear one another's burdens,' and to follow up where help is needed, giving those abstaining encouragement that they will be supported throughout the process until the next, and victorious, ceremony. After this, lead the group in a prayer of thanksgiving, bless the elements, and pass them out. This will complete your reset table.

If you have read this material, believe it to be true, and God is nudging you toward a desire to share it with your group, then pay close attention to your homework, love your brothers and sisters, and trust in God to empower you to teach and lead with conviction and passion. If you do, I guarantee you will see amazing results! I have never administrated over one of these ceremonies without marveling at what the Holy Spirit accomplishes in the lives of participants as He joyously exposes the cover-ups and brings supernatural healing!

Prepare by reading John 13 through 17 and 1st Corinthians 11. Witness the passion Christ showed for this, His most holy moment with the disciples—His final briefing to his soldiers prior to them embarking upon their ultimate mission in life. Then, seek Him in prayer for the wisdom, boldness, passion, and compassion you will need to facilitate His Spirit moving in your small group.

The repetitive nature of Communion provides for the regular maintenance of our spiritual and emotional health. Once we understand the true nature of why God gave us this ceremony, we are constantly reminded of the need to gather with others, confess our sins, and begin the process anew. We don't even have to wait for Communion to do that!

How He Wants to Be Known

Finally, during what we have come to call 'the High Priestly Prayer,' we find recorded the last thing Jesus did the night of His Passover just before He entered the Garden of Gethsemane. In it He beseeched His Father twice, "May they be one as You and I are one *so that the world may know You sent me.*" In John 13, He said, "The world will know you are My disciples by the love you have *for one another.*"

Jesus wanted first and foremost for us to be known as His, and also the reason He came to earth, through the same witness: the love displayed within His soma. There is nowhere better designed and ordained for bonding and love in the body than a place where deeply rooted issues come to the light, people join in prayer, wounds are healed, and His children are set free than right here at the Communion table! When truth is being taught, love is being embraced and admonishment is being shared and received, repentance is being lived out, and confession and prayer are the order of the day, there is nothing—*nothing*—more conducive to authentic Christian community. Your group of disciples, like His, will go forth into the great adventure of the faith bright-eyed and bushy-tailed: healed and ready to enjoy their citizenship in the kingdom of heaven on earth if everyone has the courage to observe a biblically observed reset table!

Chapter XIV
Bringing it Back to the Church

"Non nobis solum nati sumus.
[Not for ourselves alone are we born]."
— Marcus Tullius Cicero

Communion can be experienced to a much more effective extent in a large group after a proper understanding for it has been developed in the small group, but that must start with courageous pastors given the hierarchal structure of the modern church. If some will simply bear witness to the whole truth in an effort to see their flocks cleansed, healed, and unified—if they will but take seriously the power for good or damage this single opportunity presents, I am wholly convinced that we would begin to turn the tide on this Laodicean sleep that has overcome the church in America.

Training Worthy Administrators

The blending of the small and large formats can be accomplished if we commit to small-group fellowships, train worthy leaders for them, and make those fellowships the training grounds for the ceremony. Small group leaders, as elders, need to walk the walk of transparency and integrity before their flocks on a regular basis. If they cannot, they will be unable to react to Communion's formidable challenges with the required credibility. The standard for shepherds needs to be Paul's for himself: "Be imitators of me, just as I am also of Christ" (1 Cor. 11), and who told his disciple Timothy to commit the truths of God to 'faithful men, who would be able to teach others also' (2 Tim. 2).

Addressing those who choose to administrate the table: James warned that we should be extremely careful about considering our calling to become teachers. Those who do, set themselves up for a 'stricter judgment' than others will face (Jas. 3:1). These biblical guidelines need to be the model for the selection of small group leaders and are fully sufficient to qualify administrators of the table, seminary degrees or not.

As part of their training, small group leaders should celebrate a reset table with the pastor or a worthy administrator before leading their own groups through it. This will provide an ideal boot camp, as they will get to experience first-hand the challenges and the joys of Communion, raise the questions they themselves will be asked, see the community fostered there for their encouragement, and understand fully what they will be asking of their flocks to unleash the power of the ceremony effectively.

Removing Stifling Mandates

If the administration of Communion is to be returned to its rightful hands we must begin challenging unbiblical rules and regulations forbidding lay leaders to oversee it. Again, the New Testament models of Passover were house churches which were overseen by elders. Never are pastors or seminary degrees mentioned, and the Pharisees weren't invited to Jesus' Passover. Replacing God's liberties with men's hierarchies in this fashion was precisely the sort of thing that allowed religion to take over, caused 'the lost sheep in His Father's house,' and elicited Christ's ire toward them.

The administration of the elements, like all other gifts from God, is a matter of divine calling upon men's hearts. For example, I have always felt fully capable of administering Communion, whereas one time I baptized someone and knew immediately that was not my calling. The Bible is filled with stories of God gifting ordinary men and women to accomplish extraordinary things. In fact, it is they who are chosen above those the world would deem as worthy (1 Cor. 1:26-28). The utter failure of the Scribes and Pharisees to shepherd the House of Israel, and their counterparts today yielding such poor polling results, provides ample evidence that degrees of man mean nothing in and of themselves, and can actually prove counter-productive to God's desires.

While I am not recommending the selection of those to lead Communion be done without thought to their qualifications whatsoever, those credentials need to come in the form of spiritual anointing and through acknowledgment of the flock. Overseers and deacons have clearly set forth guidelines of character and conduct in the New Testament, and nowhere within them is it stated that a man be ordained by anyone save the Holy Spirit.

If denominational boundaries prohibit lay pastors from administering the elements, may I suggest your small group leaders be installed as elders and deacons? If all else fails, you can have someone who is ordained come join you to perform just that part of it. However, the small-group leader should still teach and oversee all activities leading up to that point. If even this is disallowed, may I suggest a new church affiliation is in order? Such Pharisaical, unbiblical, stifling policies must not be allowed to suffocate the clearly established house-to-house participation upon which the New Testament church and Christ's Passover were founded.

Chapter XV
It's up to You now

I am reminded of a regular speaker that used to come to retreats when I was with Young Life. His trademark summation on the last night of camp, after clearly sharing the gospel during the week, was to apologize to those who refused the extended hand of Jesus. He would say, "I'm sorry. I really need to apologize to some of you, for now you have no excuse for refusing God's offer of salvation as you stand before Him on judgment day. I have fully and clearly explained the Gospel to you, so if you have refused His invitation, I just need to tell you I'm sorry."

I would now ask you, what would keep you from employing this marvelous gift of God to break the spell of the superficiality, along with all its collateral damage, the polls tell us so clearly exists in the body of Christ today? I have explained it fully [in critical cases perhaps redundantly] to you, the reader—both the dangers of continued wrongful participation, along with the joys and benefits of experiencing the cleansing and healing that awaits all who will follow the biblical model. Will you be a part of renewal or continue to settle for the status quo?

Through His death, resurrection, and establishment of His Passover Jesus has placed a miraculous gift in your hands. The question becomes, will you unwrap it? It's up to you now. If you know in your spirit that this is right, then hear the words of James when he says, "Tis sin for the one who knows the right thing to do and fails to do it" (Jas. 4). Simply ask yourself how your spirit reacts to the current way it is done. Do you feel the power of life and death in it, or not? Do you exit modern observances transformed or not? Do you really feel anything at all?

Dietrich Bonhoeffer so impressed his Nazi prison guards that they risked their own lives to set up a network smuggling his writings out of Hitler's prisons shortly before he was condemned to the death camp at Flossenbürg. He created a community of believers in the most hideous and prosecutorial environments imaginable, and he did it in a way that so confounded and impressed his captors that many went to him for counseling concerning what to do with a Reich they, too, had come to see as evil. Hitler saw to it his sentence of death by hanging was carried out just days before the Allies liberated the camp. According to witnesses, he went with peace in his heart and no anger whatsoever shown towards his prosecutors.

When it comes to Christian community, and a man who set the highest standard of what it meant to be a shepherd of the flock, history has provided few who have proven worthy to loose his sandals. In his treatise on Christian community, *Life Together*, such a man wrote:

> The day of the Lord's Supper is an occasion of joy for [God's] community. Reconciled in their hearts with God and the brethren... [the congregation] is given new fellowship with God and men. The fellowship of The Lord's Supper is the superlative fulfillment of [the] fellowship...Here the community has reached its goal. Here joy in Christ and His community is complete. The life of the Christian community under the Word has reached its perfection in the sacrament [words in brackets mine].

This spiking event—this exclamation point—this ancient path of house-to-house fellowship full of conviction and the power to heal, will take you and your small-group fellowship places you have never been. It is indeed 'the superlative fulfillment of the fellowship.' It may come slowly, and certainly not without its share of difficulties, requiring radical changes in thinking, teaching, and practice—things people always fear. Yet isn't radical change what the church desperately needs to awaken men from this cursed weakness, sickness, and sleep?

Chapter XV

Press on, endure, and get ready for that new thing God is always doing! Reset tables will open doors to closer fellowship along with numerous opportunities for evangelism and discipleship. A final visit to the rules of the 12-Step is in order here:

> Having had a spiritual awakening as the result of these steps, we tried to carry this message to addicts and to practice these principles in all our affairs.

I sincerely hope that you have had a spiritual awakening to the awesome power of Communion, you will try to carry this message to the fellowships of believers in your sphere of influence, and you will practice these principles every time you partake. I hope some of you will follow Jane's lead and actually challenge your pastors to restore the balance of truth and grace.

When you think about it, evangelists are nothing more than people who have become profoundly changed by some revelation of God in their lives and then want to share that revelation with others. For the sake of the church, I hope you will become an evangelist for the no-longer *Pass(ed) over Table*. What do you have to lose? Take a chance on spreading the word and help the 'life of your Christian community reach its perfection in the Sacrament!'

Acknowledgements

Thanks to Cecil Murphey for all his support, both prayer and financial, to Michael Wells of Abiding Life Ministries for his wisdom and showing me what an authentic disciple was to look like, to the Rhema Men's Group from Denver, Colorado, my 'church,' that has been such a large part of my spiritual development since 2017, to my wife Tammi for standing by me through the turbulent seas she has endured as I wrestled with religion and found the kingdom, to Eddie Jones, my publishing guide and friend who unselfishly guides me through the self-publishing process and, last but by no means least, to 'the group' from Columbine High School Young Life that was so much a part of the discovery and development of all you read in these pages.

Appendix A: Leadership Teaching & Preparation Outline

To administrators of the Table: I am available through my website [www.theawakenedchristianman.org] or via email [Reconnectedchurch@gmail.com] to help you in whatever way I can. Have the courage to stand up for truth, prepare well, lead and teach well, trust in God, love your flock, and you will do well!

I. Establish the biblical 'house-to-house' environment:
   a. Passover of Exodus: Families gathered in small gr:ups behind closed doors
   b. Jesus' Passover: Opened only to His spiritual family behind closed doors
      i. Discuss spiritual family per Matt. 12:36-50
   c. The Pentecostal church: broke bread house to house while gathering in the temple for services

II. Establish a small-group environment with plenty of time:
   a. Be conducive to embracing the love and considering the admonishments of the Spirit

   i. Review and comment on Jesus' balanced message of love and admonishment (John 13-18) and Paul's (1 Cor. 11 Communion instruction)
    1. It's about so much more than grace!
  b. People won't open up in large groups full of strangers
   i. Trust built through small groups best for transparency
  c. It takes time to teach properly and to engage in individual prayer and small group confessional

III. Discuss warnings to believers and unbelievers in Paul's instructions:
  a. Unbelievers: 1 Cor. 11:23-26 – Must be able to proclaim Jesus' name to participate [make sure they know they are welcome to observe!]
  b. Believers: vs. 27-31 – Must not come with hard hearts or covered-up, rationalized sin
   i. Causing the spiritual weakness, sickness, and sleep we see in church today
  c. Here is where we deal with and break such patterns
   i. Review foundational areas of sin (per Chapter IV)

IV. The Matthew 5 Alternative:
   a. This is where we will 'here remember' what God or our brother has against us if we will be open to a thorough self-exam before God and man
   b. What to do if kingdom business needs to be tended to
      i. Leave our offering at the Altar [abstain], go take care of business, and return in victory!
         1. Review the responsibilities of the fellowship concerning follow-up
   c. The only sin at the table is taking unworthily, not abstinence [unless that is done to ignore responsibilities to confront and confess]
      i. Encourage abstinence and participation as *both* being victories if done in the interest of becoming real with self and God
   d. Why was Communion given to us as a regular ceremony: to keep dealing with our sinful natures and ongoing propensities to rationalize and cover-up

V. Individual prayer and corporate confession and prayer [recommend 30 minutes]:
   a. Individual prayer: Time to open souls to God's conviction
      i. Not time for intercession for others, but deliberate opening to examination by the Spirit to discern what He or others may have against us'

- ii. Make copies of the prayer recorder [Appendix] and ask participants to review verses there before going to prayer
    1. Encourage everyone to record *everything* the Spirit brings to mind. If they will not, cover-ups are indicated
- b. Corporate confession and prayer: Stress the uniqueness of James 5:16:
    - i. Forgiveness through vertical confession, healing through horizontal
        1. Must at least begin to confront issues on prayer recorder or admit rationalizing and denial
            - a. If people can't confront encourage abstinence
        2. God will not heal if we refuse to confess to others

VI. Miscellaneous other teachings [best done in prior studies in the interest of time and retention abilities of your flock]:
- a. The *soma*: are we aiding the body in its journey or holding it back?
- b. What to do in corporate settings when warnings are not given
- c. Prodigal Son analogy

VII. Partaking of the Elements:
- a. Final review of the importance of being real with God
    - i. Abstinence and participation are *both* victories if done with the right heart
    - ii. Solemnly warn any from eating and drinking judgment upon themselves if they know they have kingdom business to attend to and are ignoring it
- b. Importance of the accountability, assistance, and prayer of the fellowship for the return of those struggling in victory

Appendix B
Prayer Recorder

Heb. 4:12-13: "For the word of God is living and active and sharper than any two-edged sword...able to judge the thoughts and intentions of the heart...All things are open and laid bare to the eyes of Him..."

Ps. 139:23-24: "Search me, O God, and know my heart; try me and know my anxious thoughts; and see if there be any hurtful way in me."

1 Cor. 4:4-5: "Wait until the Lord comes, who will both bring to light the things hidden in the darkness and disclose the motives of men's hearts."

Ps. 90:8: "You have placed our iniquities before You; our secret sins in the light of Your presence."

A love I need to embrace:

_____
_____
_____
_____

198 • Appendix B

Admonishments I need to consider:

_____
_____
_____
_____

Cover-ups and sinful practices I've not confessed:

_____
_____
_____
_____

Amends/kingdom business to attend to:

_____
_____
_____
_____

Encouragement/admonishment for others:

_____
_____
_____
_____

Appendix C: The Communion/12-Step Comparison

1. We admitted we were powerless over [insert your issue] - that our lives had become unmanageable. *[We were dead in our trespasses and sins (Eph. 2:1), and realized Jesus is the only way to be forgiven (Eph. 1:7). We have no power over sin apart from this truth].*

2. Came to believe that a power greater than ourselves could restore us to sanity. *[If we use the Communion table the way it was meant, we are restored to sanity from the insanity that self-deception and rationalization of sin causes (Matt. 6:23, 2 Cor. 10:5)].*

3. Made a decision to turn our will and our lives over to the care of God as we understood Him. *[At the Communion table, we symbolically eat Jesus' body and drink His blood, thereby turning ourselves fully over to His care (John 6:53-56)].*

4. Made a searching and fearless moral inventory of ourselves. *[We are to let God examine us (1 Cor. 4:4) and examine ourselves, and so eat and drink (1 Cor. 11:27-28)]*

5. Admitted to God, to ourselves, and to another human being the exact nature of our wrongs. *[Confession not just vertically but horizontally as well (1 Cor. 4:4, Jas. 5:16), bringing healing and keeping a clear conscience both before God and men (Acts 24:16)].*

6. Were entirely ready to have God remove all these defects of character. *[Removing hard hearts toward changes that are needed (Jas. 1:5-8, Luke 18:13-14)].*

7. Humbly asked Him to remove our shortcomings. *[Time of vertical confession (1 John. 1:9, 2 Cor. 12:8-9)].*

8. Made a list of all persons we had harmed, and became willing to make amends to them all. *[Communion action: Matthew 5 Alternative (Matt. 5:23-24, Prov. 6:1-5)].*

9. Made direct amends to such people wherever possible, except when to do so would injure them or others. *[Ditto rule #8].*

10. Continued to take personal inventory and, when we were wrong, promptly admitted it. *[Communion maintains our faith, which is why we are to partake regularly (1 Cor. 11:26, Acts 2:42)].*

11. Sought through prayer and meditation to improve our conscious contact with God as we understood Him, praying only for knowledge of His will for us and the power to carry that out. *[Why we are to 'abide*

in Christ' (John 15:5, 2 Cor. 10:5) and to act on His convictions we receive at the table (John 15:10, 14)].

12. Having had a spiritual awakening as the result of these steps, we tried to carry this message to others and practice these principles in all our affairs. *[Why we are to 'bear fruit' by properly partaking and administrating the table. We need to be biblical Communion 'evangelists' to all others in the house of God, making true disciples through the proper observation of God's holiest of all ceremonies (Matt. 28:19-20)].*